Tough to Follow Acts

Seventy-five monologs for teens

Shirley Ullom

MERIWETHER PUBLISHING LTD.
Colorado Springs, Colorado

Meriwether Publishing Ltd., Publisher
P.O. Box 7710
Colorado Springs, CO 80933

Editor: Arthur L. Zapel
Typesetting: Elisabeth Hendricks
Cover design: Janice Melvin

© Copyright MM Meriwether Publishing Ltd.
Printed in the United States of America
First Edition

Library of Congress Cataloging-in-Publication Data

Ullom, Shirley, 1938–
    Tough acts to follow : seventy-five monologs for teens / Shirley Ullom.
    p. cm.
    ISBN: 1-56608-057-6 (paper)
    1. Monologues. 2. Teenagers--Drama. I. Title.

PN2080.U45 2000
812'.54--dc21

00-024678

1 2 3 4 5 6 7 8   00 01 02 03

Dedication

For my brother, who likes the kid in me, and all my female
friends who have supported my writing, made me laugh and keep
a heart young enough to write for teenagers — especially Mom,
Naomi and my "Ya-Ya" friends ...

Preface

In *Tough Acts to Follow* I've considered all the kids I've had in my classes — casts of thousands! I've tried to think of their quirks, their idiosyncrasies — those weird, twisted qualities that make them *teenagers!* The one trait that makes a teen stand apart from the rest of society is humor ... sometimes it gets a little much, a little too smutty, a little cruel, but it's part of their makeup, their personality and their style! In these monologs I've tried to capture some of this humor ... okay, a *lot* of this humor!

I've also tried to hit on other teenage attitudes, lifestyles and problems — death, divorce, eating disorders, gangs, violence in schools, drop-outs, abusive relationships, etc. But fear not, there are lots of pages left for the fun topics! In these monologs, I've tried to reveal the teenager as I see him or her after my years (no, I won't reveal my age) of working with them — honest, sincere, outspoken, rude, outrageous, fearless, inquisitive ... and most of the time delightful!

I hope these writings stir up some awareness — make teenagers stop and think — and, of course, I want teens to have a great time performing these monologs. I had fun writing them for you, so enjoy. Put some hormonal teenage breath into these characters, 'cause after all, they're *Tough Acts to Follow!*

Contents

Girls or Guys

About the Author

Introduction

Kids, this book's really for you. Do I make fun of the teenage dilemma? *Sure!* Do I exaggerate your flaws? *Sure!* Do I poke fun at your weaknesses? *Sure!* But if you can't laugh at yourself ...

So, just kick back and have a super time with these monologs. Remember, if you need to add or subtract stuff ... change a name, place, or circumstance, add a few new slang words (G-rated, of course) ... *Go for it!* After all, I can't do everything!

Guys

Beached Babes

I'm set now, what a job! The primo work experience ... numero uno workplace ... lifeguard at an awesome beach! All the guys are sooo jealous. They said I got it because my rich Uncle Jerome's a city commissioner! Hey, I earned my badges, swam my butt off, passed the test ... begged Uncle Jerome! OK, OK, I cheated — so sue me — but it was worth it! I'm sitting up here like the King of the Hill. Any minute those long-legged blondes will be all over me. I'll have to fight them off with a flyswatter, and I doubt I'll put up much of a fight! By the end of the season I'll be so tan, so buff, so loaded down with sexy chicks' phone numbers! I wonder if I should play hard to get; nah, I'm just going to grab some gusto — grab some excitement.

I've got my binoculars; I can spot the babes as they head my way. Oh, I'm sure I'll keep one eye on the ocean. Sure hope no kids show up and ruin my fun. I'd hate to have to actually swim out and save some little rugrat; it'd wash off my sunscreen and play havoc with my hair to actually get it wet. I've got it combed just right, so I hope the mamas on this beach keep a tight hold on their offspring. I'm not being paid to be a babysitter ... now, a babe sitter's another matter!

Where is everybody, anyway? I've been here for thirty minutes and so far not one Sun Goddess has come my way. Maybe they all sleep in — get that beauty sleep that makes them look so hot! Speaking of hot, I'm sweating already. This umbrella keeps the sun off, but it's a little muggy up here in Lifeguard Heaven! By the end of the day I'll be one well-done piece of meat. But it'll be worth a little discomfort when the sexy women start swarming around me. Maybe I'll let one fan me; one can feed me grapes; the others can wait their turn to worship at my Lifeguard Throne! Man, I've got it made; will I have stories to tell when school starts. I'll be *the Man!*

3

Oh look, a big bus is pulling up ... looks like ... yes, it's really my day ... it's filled with females! A busload of women landing on my beach on my *first* day! I've only got one thing to say to you Mighty Neptune, God of the Sea ... thank ya, thank ya, thank ya! Wow, blondes, brunettes, and redheads ... enough to make a guy color blind. They're unloading ... let's get out the old spyglasses and get a close up. I'll just feast these eyes on luscious girl tidbits! Ah, oh ... what's this? The first *Baywatch* babe off the bus is a little on the wrong side of thirty and well, hefty ... let's just see ... hummm ... oh, my ... that's more woman than I bargained for and in Mom's age bracket ... oops, more Golden Oldies. What does it say on that bus? Oh, no ... Mature Woman's Healthy Exercise Club — Swim to Be Thin! Instead of chicks, my beach's being invaded by a busload of bigger-than-life mature ladies!

And they've got beach towels and big lunch boxes — that means they're here for the day! What if I have to save one of them? I'm not Hercules, ya know! Well, I'm not a quitter. I just hope the guys don't show up today; after all my braggin', I'd really be in for it! I'll just shape up and do my job. Everybody's got a right to the beach, I guess, and I doubt they'll drown. They look like floaters to me! But I'm sure not rubbing lotion on *those* backs! I won't be getting any phone numbers ... won't need any ... except 911! I should have known this job wasn't going to pan out like I dreamed ... only in the movies. Uncle Jerome didn't do me such a big favor after all. The *Big* stuff's on the beach ... no doubt about it. And I thought this job was just too good to be true!

Billy's Gone

I didn't see it coming ... my best friend committed suicide last week! He was only seventeen ... had his best years ahead. He was an A student — liked by everyone — even Old Man Swinkle who hates everyone liked Billy!

I feel so guilty ... I talked to him that evening. He sounded OK ... Oh, he was a little down that Jan had dumped him, but not that down. He hadn't been going to baseball practice — said his arm hurt. He never had much to say at lunch, but heck, who can talk with cafeteria food stuck to the roof of your mouth? I know he was under a lot of pressure at home; his dad was a perfectionist and expected, no demanded, the same from his son. I don't really think Billy ever got to relax at home. He was always doing chores, polishing up his homework or practicing his pitching. He was never one to complain; I think he kept it all bottled up inside. I suggested once that he might talk to the school counselor. Mr. West was an OK guy. But Billy said, "We Suttons solve our own problems." And I guess he did — but the old "permanent solution for a temporary problem" keeps going through my mind. I don't know how I'll make it through my senior year without Billy. We've been best friends since fourth grade — went through Scouts together. (I'm sorry to say that's where Billy learned to make the hangman's knot!) Of course, Billy's dad wasn't satisfied till he became Eagle Scout ... I was just in it for the cookies.

We had a memorial assembly for Billy — he was class president, first chair trumpet, outstanding athlete, and shoo-in for valedictorian! And the question that has everybody running scared — if a guy like that can't take the stress, what about us mortal men? I don't know if there was a note ... his father won't speak to me — like it's my fault. He didn't approve of Billy having any friends or distractions. He was a hard man, but I know in his own way, he loved his son and was proud of him — I saw the look of fatherly pride on his face when Billy pitched a no-hitter. Now, he just looks broken — hollow — a man without a purpose ... a man without a son.

I suppose we'll never know what caused our super guy Billy to take his life — I do know our school's brought in grief counselors and is trying to get the word out to kids and parents — if you're depressed, talk to somebody. Don't try to solve your problems alone. If you know somebody who's down all the time or withdrawing from his old life or talking about suicide — bring in some help ... don't wait. Maybe if we'd all tried a little harder ... listened closer ... put in more time, we'd still have Billy. It's too late for my friend, but it might not be for somebody else — maybe someone you know.

Blinded by My Dates

You guys have all been there ... waiting for the door to open on your blind date ... expecting to see a young Cindy Crawford and instead gazing at Frankenstein's twin sister! I don't know why, but for some reason I'm always the fall guy who gets sucked into taking out everybody's cousin from out of town, sister's roommate from camp, or used-to-be next-door neighbor who's all grown up now! Every time I go on one of these "pity" dates I make a solemn vow — promise myself — *never again!* But, because I have a soft heart and I'm an easy pushover for a sob story, and because my dating calendar is usually blank — I give in at the cost of my self-respect, my ego, my eyesight and once again tackle the "blind date"!

And man, have I been blinded! I've spent long evenings with these unseen, great-personality cast-offs — women who possessed every kind of female flaw! Stephen King could use my diary for research material! I've dated gals with weird shapes — pear-shaped or square-shaped is OK for diamonds, but not for chicks! Some of these never-before-seen dates have smelled bad, had facial tics, and digestive problems. I've been pushed into escorting bowls-full-of-jelly-types and skeleton-girls from the closet. Why do I do it? Why can't I just say no? 'Cause I'm a lily-livered weakling, that's why — a gutless wimp with a dating death wish!

Only once has it been a good experience ... only once did I smile instead of upchuck at the end of the devastating date ... only once was it a cute girl with all her own teeth, a body to die for, breath and armpits both fresh as a mountain breeze! But it was too good to last ... she was just passing through, needed an escort for the evening, had a steady guy at home. But it felt so super taking out a girl I could actually look at and swallow fries with at the same time! This one good moment has actually given me hope — raised my level of expectation for these sight-unseen dates.

No matter how often I say I'll never date "blindly" again, I know I will.

7

Whenever someone calls with two girls on their hands; whenever an extra male is needed to even out a fun evening; whenever the original date has sneaked a peek at the "surprise" girl and had to call 911 — I'll be there! Yep! I'll step into a video arcade and come out with slicked-back hair and shades that are so heavily tinted that anybody looks good! Look — faster than the O.J. trial ... more powerful than Starr's report ... able to climb anthills in geeky high-top shoes ... it's a nerd ... it's an old flame ... no, it's Super Blind Date Guy!

Bunch of Misfits

If you saw the guys I hang with — I guess you might say we're kind of "off-the-wall"! We're not the pretty-boy girl catchers; we haven't outgrown acne and Lucky Charms! We barely shave! We're not the jock itch crowd either — we don't bat, dribble (well, maybe a little soup), or run touchdowns, but we do spin a mean yo-yo! Yet we can't be called geeks — we're not smart enough to fit in that group. We're just a bunch of guys caught in the middle — somewhere between Leonardo DiCaprio and that Urkell kid! We're slightly below average, but with hopes of outgrowing our shortcomings! OK, OK, we're a pack of losers ... and too thick-skulled to know it. Ya happy now? But ya know what? We don't care; we're happy with ourselves; we've got a life!

Take Ralphie, for instance. He's the video games superstar — nobody can beat him at anything! He's the king of all the combat games — a real blood and guts guru, but you know, he prefers a simple game where two monkeys try to out-fox each other. In fact, he's so obsessed with this "monkey" thing, he bought a big, inflatable banana that hangs from the ceiling of his room! He makes chimp noises now, and scratches himself! He used to like Dr. Pepper ... now, it's banana juice! I suppose we ought to get the kid some help, but we just keep bringing him bananas!

Then we have Hank, a real car freak. At any given time there's enough grease under his fingernails to fry a dozen eggs. His clothes are spotted with oil, and he always gives off the charming aroma of dead gas ... yep, old Hank's a real lady's man! His bed is made from a real car frame — has the steering wheel and tires intact. His walls are plastered with ... what else — car posters! He's head of the class in auto mechanics — can't say the same for English and Hygiene 112!

Chuckie, alias Garbage Gut, is one of my best pals. He has his head in the refrigerator most of the time ... not to get cool — there's nothing cool about Chuckie! No, he's got the Amana open because he's stuffing

9

his face ... his tummy ... his chubby legs ... you get it — the Chuckster loves to eat! While he's finishing one meal, he starts on the appetizer for the next! You don't see this kid without a sandwich in his pocket and an Almond Joy in his mouth. His school lunchbox has wheels! In kindergarten Chuckie brought his weekly supply of graham crackers in a Hefty bag!

So ya see, I wasn't puttin' ya on ... my friends aren't your usual run-of-the-mill teenagers. Not that there's anything wrong with being different. We just say we have character. That's what the girls say — "You're characters!" But girls — that's another subject. I couldn't truthfully say that our dating scores are any higher than our GPAs — both are below average. But somewhere out there lurk some chicks in the same category — not all females are tens! We'd settle for a few six-and-a-halfs! Believe it or not, sometimes we get serious — say we're going to shape up, straighten up ...grow up! At times like this Ralphie's willing to cut back on the banana juice and quit scratching in public; Hank looks up a manicurist in the Yellow Pages; and Chuckie takes his head out of the trough long enough to belch and say he'll go "cold turkey" ... if somebody throws in the giblets!

But to tell the truth, I don't see any changes in sight. We like ourselves ... our lifestyles. Sure, we'll probably come around someday — face off with reality, but for now, leave us alone. We're a bunch of numbskulls, but so what? We're happy!

Chin Up, Buddy

Come on, Buddy ... look, I brought your favorite — Milk-Bone. Here's some water, Old Boy ... you know you've got to eat. I know, I know, you keep missing Justin. Well, he was my best friend, too, you know. Yeah, he was quite a guy ... look here's a picture of the two of you with your Bears hats on, and here you are with Justin in his old Chevy. You guys rode lots of miles in that old buggy ... me, too. We've had lots of good times, Buddy, the three of us ... you're one great hunting dog, Fella. As Labs go, you're tops. But you're gonna get sick if you don't eat. Do you want to go for a run? Here's your leash. Come on, Buddy, you love to get out in the field and suck in the fresh air. Here, just one little bite of Milk-Bone. I broke off just a little taste ... here, I'll try it ... ummm, good!

You know everybody's worried about you ... Dr. Shafer checked you last night, right? I know you wonder about all the crying and why all the strangers are here ... and most of all I know you wonder why Justin hasn't come home. Well, Pal, I hate to be the one to tell you, but Justin's not coming home. Oh, God, I can't understand it myself ... and I don't know how to explain it so it'll make sense to you. Remember night before last when Justin and I were going to that party? I heard him talking to you about it ... explaining about all the good-looking chicks who'd be there. He told you about Julie — the one with the great legs and sexy eyes. Yeah, see that got your interest, Buddy. And I saw Justin scratch your ears and toss you a couple of extra Milk-Bones ... he said he'd see you after midnight ... and he didn't mean to lie to you, Buddy, he thought he'd be coming home. He didn't know when he and Julie got into that car with Mark that it'd be their last ride. I tried to stop them. I told him Mark'd been putting away too many and shouldn't be driving. I tried to get him and Julie to come with me ... but Jennifer and Julie were best friends ... and separating a teenage girl from her best friend is impossible! ... Now I've been separated from mine forever ... you, too,

Old Fella! ... I know "friends don't let friends drive drunk" ... I followed them to the car ... made a real pest of myself. Mark finally shoved me away. Justin said, "It'll be OK, Chris, I'll see you tomorrow. We'll take Buddy out hunting." But he didn't ... and there are no tomorrows for the three of us, Buddy. It was a semi ... and it was instant ... he didn't suffer ... just us, Buddy. We're going to suffer the rest of our lives. I tried to stop him ... God, I should have pulled him out of that car. I should have grabbed the keys and thrown them in the river. I feel so guilty ... and now I don't have a friend and you're in this empty room waiting for someone who'll never again say, "Come here, Buddy, you old Sport!"

But we have to carry on, Buddy; Justin wouldn't want you to grieve. Tell you what, I'll come over this afternoon — it'll have to be after three. I have to go to something called a funeral. You're lucky, Buddy, at least you don't have to carry your best friend to his grave! But I'll be here, I promise ... and we'll go running ... go to Justin's favorite places. Atta' boy, Buddy. See you *can* still eat ... and there's that lopsided grin ... we're gonna make it, Pal. Life's never going to be the same for us, though ... 'cause our best buddy's gone.

Crush on Miss Perkins

You can have your cheerleaders, your drill team girls, your jazz dancers … just let me sit in sophomore English and drool at the feet of Miss Perkins. This woman is a goddess, sent to me from on high — not to learn participles, gerunds and prepositions (propositions, maybe …). No, she was a special gift; I just lucked out. Half the sophomores got Old Lady Dumby — she hides in closets drinking 7-Up and munching crackers. When she comes out, she smells like a cross between Preparation H and death! So, I thank my guardian angel every day for getting me in Perkins' class.

I know it's not unusual for kids to have crushes on their teachers. In kindergarten, Smitty had a wild romantic inclination toward Miss Kline … and he didn't even mind that she had mismatched eyes and ashtray breath! Tony still has a thing for Mrs. Biles, our third grade teacher. He always sends her valentines and writes "Roses are red" poems for her. In junior high, all our hormones were too keyed-up over "real girls" to look at the over-the-hill gang. We did all take a second look at Miss Winston — fresh out of college, P.E. teacher … legs that went clear up to her nostrils!

But with Miss Perkins, it was love at first sight. When I stumbled into class that first day, dreading the same old stuff — diagramming sentences (Fitting words into little boxcars turns my stomach.) … making subjects and verbs agree (Heck, I can't get my mom and dad to agree.) … double negatives (I don't see no reason for this lesson.) … and choosing the right pronoun. (To whom it may concern: Get a life!) I sat in the back row with all the other happy D students hoping to catch a few winks (from either the Sandman or Jessica Farley)! But just as I was getting all slouched down (surefire method of invisibility) I took one more gander around the room, before letting my brain kick into nothingsville. She said not a word, but went straight to her work … wrote the assignment on the board — called Tommy a jerk! And I heard her exclaim — her smile out-of-sight

— "Get your work done on time, or your grade's going to bite!"

So, that's how it started — my Perkins' passion. I suffered through the rest of the day … but was amply rewarded …'cause I'm the lucky guy who gets to spend the last hour of my day in the presence of beauty, wit, intelligence … and legs that make male teenage eyeballs whirl like slot machines! I've done all of the kiss-up tactics to become a complete suck-up. I don't care that my friends call me Wimp Basket, Drool Baby and Kissy Kissy. I'm just glad my little tricks worked! Miss Perkins lets me take up the homework (because I bought her a bouquet of daisies that I picked … right beside the sign that said "Stop and smell the roses — *don't* pick them!") I'd walk through alligator droppings to have Miss Wonderful's undivided attention for five minutes. But my best kiss-up caper was to volunteer to help Miss Bonnie (Cindy Crawford) Perkins grade papers after class. I bought her a cutsie red pen with an apple on top for Valentine's Day. She fell for it. So, every Tuesday and Thursday you'll find me in room 212, feet propped up, Perkins-bought Pepsi in hand, red pen in the other … red inking all my friends' and enemies' English papers! Would I cheat? No way … this is not about raising my grade (or Billy's … or Todd's …) or helping my fellow man. I'm doing it to spend time with the woman of my dreams … my shining example of feminine beauty … my electrifying English teacher! Yeah, I guess you could really say I've got it bad. I have a major crush on Miss Perkins.

Dogs Are More Loyal Than Girls

Nobody's ever said "Babes are a man's best friend"! And there's a very good reason — it's not true! Dogs, canines, ruff-ruffs — there's where real loyalty lies. Would Suzie Harris ever bring in your newspaper? Bet you'd never talk Cami Peterson into bringing in your slippers in her sharp, little teeth. Girls — they won't roll over and play dead ... aren't good at fetching sticks ...

Dogs are trustworthy, and a fire hydrant is all they need to be happy! And if you happen to forget their birthday, they don't whine and have all their girlfriends send you hate mail. You can tell Fido a secret and it won't be the headline in the school newspaper's gossip column. You don't have to take a mutt to the most expensive restaurant in town so they can brag to their friends. A bow-wow doesn't care if you hang out with the guys and play a little football. Old Rover doesn't give a hoot if you have the slickest car in the parking lot — he just wants you to have wheels to cart home the Kibbles and Bits!

Whoever said it's a dog-eat-dog world probably just got dumped by a female. No four-legged creature's going to give you the kiss-off because she found someone better. It doesn't take much to get the old heave-ho from a modern chick, but a dog's your pal for life. To keep a girl happy, you've gotta shower her with presents and flowers. A canine loves you if you scratch his ears! Females want you to like their friends — even the giggly ones with their snooty noses in the air! Your doggie doesn't care who you like as long as you keep dishin' up the Alpo! Girls want you to compliment their clothes, their hair, their personality — all Rin Tin Tin wants you to say is, "Gravy Train!" You're really in trouble if your main date catches you talking to another member of the opposite sex — they're so possessive ... while a pooch will forgive you petting another mongrel if you toss him a couple of Milk Bones!

A dog doesn't yak for hours on the phone; doesn't get lipstick on your collar; doesn't eat all your popcorn at the movies and doesn't have a father who fingerprints you before you leave for a date with "Daddy's Little Girl"!

So, when they say this world's "going to the dogs" ... I'm thinkin' that's not so bad. Picture this: you've had a hard day at school, you need a retreat — some space to call your own, and you need a sympathetic ear to listen to your problems. Let me tell you there's not a girl in the universe who'd sit down next to you, look up at you with those sad beagle eyes and drool all over your Nikes while you watch the Raiders' game!

Dream Girl

Since I was two years old I've been madly in love with Olivia Delpino. when she bit my ear in preschool and I had to have stitches, I knew she was special. When she threw up on my shoe in first grade, I knew she would have a big impact on my life — I still have the stained shoe! In third grade she kicked my shins and returned the box of valentine candy that cost me six weeks' allowance. In middle school her locker was only three down from mine ... I could touch it whenever I wanted ... if Olivia wasn't around. We were assigned to the same science group. I got to hold the frog while she stabbed and ripped the poor dead creature to shreds. Did I mention that Olivia has a cruel streak? She has blackened more eyes, bloodied more noses, done more bruising than the "Rock"! She's very insulting, a big backstabber, world's nosiest gossip — and those are just a few of her more endearing qualities! She's selfish and pushy; she's rude and demanding; she's grouchy and snooty — but ya just gotta love her!

I'm not sure why I have this Olivia obsession. I'm not the geekiest guy in school — girls can look at me without goggles. My friends are always trying to set me up with a *nice* girl — trying to con me into forgetting Olivia! Forget her? Sure, I'll forget her when I go home with all A's ... when school lunch starts tasting like real food ... when teachers start treating boys as well as they do girls ... *then* I'll forget Olivia!

Now that we're in high school, she's actually softened a little. I opened the door for her last week and she didn't slam my fingers when she banged it shut. She refrained from kicking my butt yesterday when I stooped to pick up the notebook she'd dropped — I'm beginning to think there's real hope for our future! But for now, I just keep looking at the pictures I have in my room. Thanks to my photography class and zoom lens, I have some outstanding Olivia shots. I do wish she'd smiled in just *one* of them. She'd have looked more like a cover girl, too, if she'd untangled her hair and unclenched her fists! Now, don't get me wrong, my beloved didn't pose for these photos — I had to catch her off-guard!

17

Had she seen me snapping, clicking, zooming ... I'd be wearing my Kodak as a nose ornament! Yes, my secret love's a little camera shy.

I know some of you are saying "This guy's nuts!" "A real cuckoo bird!" And perhaps you're right, but then you haven't met my Olivia! You haven't seen her snake-like eyes light up ... her bright little teeth glint in the sun. You haven't heard her raspy, boisterous voice whine out, "Quit looking at me or I'll twist your stupid neck so hard your eyes will pop into the gutter!" So you see, you can't judge me or my taste in females 'cause you don't know Olivia, my dream girl!

Express Yourself

You've all been through it — wobbly knees, palms sweating, throat drier than your minister's last sermon, heart pounding louder than the one in the "Tell Tale Heart," bladder ready to explode ... because you have to give *a speech!* The nationwide survey that proved people's number one fear is speaking in front of an audience (Number 2 is death) is right on the money! I'd rather eat rattlesnake innards, walk in bird droppings ... barefoot ... lick cobwebs, rinse my hair in the toilet — I hate giving speeches!

I think only gutsy, loudmouthed, lip-flappin' kids should have to perform. I don't think it's fair to make a guy who's mindin' his own business, doing what he's told, not bothering anyone stand and deliver! I know, I've heard all the helpful hints — pretend your audience is in their underwear! I really want to talk to a group in their almost birthday suits ... what pervert came up with that one? Or I could just look over the tops of their heads, if looking the audience in the eye makes me nervous. But I find tops of heads anything but comforting ... I'm not into spikes, braids, and dandruff. So, none of the old standbys work. Nothing makes me feel at ease when twenty-five sets of beady eyes are gazing my way. Sure, I know the other speakers aren't really listening to me — they're too busy writing their own last-minute outline, or being grateful they've already given their speech or busily carving their initials in the desk. Even this lack of interest from my audience doesn't help.

I will admit our speech teacher *tries* to ease us into it. First we get to be with a partner. Next, we artistically draw and hold up pictures. (When your audience is looking at your illustration, they aren't looking at you!) Then, we graduate to objects ... another crutch to take the staring mass's attention away from the embarrassed face of the speaker! But I don't care how many toilet seats I hold up, or how cute my baby picture was, I can still feel all those eyeballs aimed at me! One girl was so physically ill (upchucked in the wastebasket four times) we boys had to put our

19

heads on our desks and close our eyes so she could speak. It worked ... Maria talked like a magpie and we got a much-needed nap!

I don't mind the research — with the Internet the world's information's at my grubby little computer-trained fingertips! I like organizing my outline and note cards; finding a clever quote or joke for my introduction is a piece of cake. It's no sweat to gather up audio-visual material, but that old "a picture's worth a thousand words" doesn't cut it in this class! And last, I never forget to practice ... I know what makes perfect! So, what's the big holdup? What's giving me the night sweats ... makin' me feel like a caffeine freak? It's the *delivery*. I have the perfect package — outline, A.V., practice sessions, perfect timing — the whole spiel. Then, I ruin it all by giving the blasted speech.

And, of course, our instructor's one tough macaroon. She would have given Abe a C on his little Gettysburg talk! Kennedy's "Ask not what your country ..." would have been ripped by Ms. Speechaholic! She would have hit the lever on the guillotine when the *Tale of Two Cities* dude started with "'Tis a far, far better thing I do ..." So, you see what we're up against? And it's a required course ... otherwise we'd all be taking Basket Weaving 103! Well, gotta go ... it's about my turn to get up and make a complete fool of myself ... my turn to give another speech!

Gang's All Here

I've got a tough decision to make, and I've got to make it soon. Do I want to be a gang member or not? I know, I've read all the statistics for gang members — the percentage of deaths, drop-outs and those ending up behind prison walls. We've had cops and ex-gang members talk to our class and the message is loud and clear — *Don't join a gang!* But these do-gooders don't know the rest of the story. They don't know the pressure put on likely gang candidates. They don't know the threats, the fear if you decide not to wear the colors. I'm not saying I'll be killed or have my house burned down, but to turn your back on *the gang* is not going to get you a Mr. Nice Guy award. It's more likely to get you shoved in the halls, your tires slit, your windshield smashed. Yes, it takes guts to stand up to the Mini-Mafia and say, "I choose *not* to serve!"

But on the other hand, if you choose to join the gang *du jour*, there are some benefits. You have great camaraderie; you've instantly inherited blood brothers (and sometimes sisters) ... of course, you have to survive the rigid initiation first. These new friends will sit by you at lunch, stand by you in a fight, and you'll never feel like an outsider again. This is the main attraction — kids who have no home life are attracted like magnets to this kind of warm environment. Perhaps if it was easier to make the team or write for the school paper, some of us wouldn't feel this need to join something we know is wrong ... just to get some type of recognition. Nobody likes to feel left out, so when an invitation comes for a loner to join a gang, he often jumps at it just to carve a niche for himself ... to fit in ... someplace.

Well, I've still got a decision to make. Mom would be against it, but she'll never know. She works two shifts at McDonalds. My cousin, Marcos, has been in a gang for two years. He says it's cool ... but I'm not so sure. He's on probation for shoplifting and stealing a car, and he's all but dropped out of school. He makes fun of me, but I like school; my grades are good, and Mrs. Brown says I've got an excellent chance at a scholarship if I keep my nose clean. Then, too, there's my ace in the hole — I could go to a little town in Oklahoma that never heard of gangs and live with my Aunt Marissa. It's OK with Mom; she knows her sister would take good care of me ... maybe I could play a little basketball there. I'd never get a chance to play here, and I'm pretty good. I'd hate to leave my home, my mom, and some of my good classes. It's a tough decision ... but I think I'll give my aunt a call. And I'm going to do it right now 'cause when all's said and done, I really don't want to be pushed into joining a gang!

Gotta Be a Cowboy

I don't want to be a rock star, a lawyer, a stock broker, or an accountant (like dear old Dad). I'm not interested in politics, medicine or the ministry. Sports, teaching, nor the military turns me on. Forget about blue-collar work — I want to be a cowboy!

I know you think I'm kidding … that I haven't completely recycled my cowboy/Indian childhood fantasies. Well, you're wrong; I've known since I wore chaps over my Pampers I wanted to be a bandana-wearin', gun-totin' cowboy. Mom kept saying I'd outgrow it. She told that to the Humane Society after I'd rounded up and *branded* all the little "doggies" in the neighborhood! My mother was pretty concerned when I insisted on having a horse stall in my room and bales of hay for chairs … when I took my lunch in saddlebags … when the only animals crackers I'd eat were shaped like horses. I'm sixteen and I still sleep in cowboy and Indian jammies! I rode a stick horse till I was thirteen, and old Ruffles is still hidden in the back of my closet!

While other kids were playing T-ball and video games, Ruffles and I were watching old westerns. I've got all the Roy Rogers and Gene Autry tapes … I sing "I'm Back in the Saddle Again" while I shower … and "Happy Trails to You" while I'm cleanin' my room. (Luckily for people who have an ear for good singing, I don't do either one very often!) I have autographed pictures of Roy, Gene, Hopalong Cassidy and John Wayne. (I know he's not all cowboy, but he's close enough!) I used to argue with my cousin who'd have come out ahead in the Kentucky Derby — Trigger or Champion! Needless to say, I was downright busted when I heard that Gene Autry and Roy Rogers (King of the Cowboys) had died in the same year.

I've done some work towards my goal of becoming a cowboy. First, I had to find out where they have cows! I live in the city! I took riding lessons, visited Boot Hill at Dodge City, read all about Doc Holiday and Wyatt Earp, put my feet up on the rail at the Long Branch, had a thirstquenchin' sarsaparilla, bought an expensive, authentic cowboy hat! I also took a summer job on a dude ranch in Montana — learned to ride, rope and say "Yeehaw!" I've developed a great drawl, say "Y'all," and I'm never without my cowboy hat! So, I'm getting there! I'll make you proud, Roy!

Yep, I can see it all now ... me sacked out in the bunkhouse, jawbonin' with the other hands, talkin' trail talk! I'll eventually get my own spread, find a Dale Evans-type filly and raise some little cowpokes! No, this isn't just a dream ... it'll happen. I'm really ... *really* ... gonna be a cowboy!

Gotta Get a Girlfriend

Let's face it, there comes a time in every man's life when he needs female companionship, and for me the time has arrived. I've outgrown Legos; I don't require a sitter when my mommy's out for the evening; I buy my own underwear; I get Big Macs instead of Happy Meals at McDonalds. So you see, I'm spreading my wings and I don't want to fly solo — I want a girlfriend.

I guess you'd say I'm a late bloomer; all my friends have been playing the dating game for some time. Well, except for Wilbur who still thinks girls are guys with bumps! But I really think I'm ready now ... ready to get out there and smell the perfume. But, since I'm new at this, I'll need a game plan. I can't just swing down on a vine and grab a Jane-like chick! To tell the truth, that doesn't really sound so bad ... but where does a guy get a vine? Everything's so complicated in the civilized world.

Now, I've got to settle down and think this through — it's hard to think when the hormones are chuggin' like a Texaco gas pump! I could always go the blind date route, but I've heard too many psycho stories from guys trying that. There are lots of mirror-shatterin' females out there — and they're standin' in long lines — just waitin' for some dumb-cluck guy to blind date 'em! But not this boy — I'm finding myself a classy gal.

Now, here's my list of eligible chicks ... I'll just get on my cellular ... start at the top and work my way down till one agrees to go out with me. *(Picks up phone.)* Hello, Lindsay! *(Puts phone down.)* It didn't work ... had to hang up ... my voice sounded like Donald Duck going through puberty! Oh, it's hopeless. I'll just spend the rest of my high school years droolin' over anything in a skirt, just being a spectator as the Babe Parade goes right past me, leaving me sitting on the curb ... alone.

Hey, look over there ... it's Kristy Holmes ... she's waving at me! Come on, hand, wave back — you can do it! Oh my gosh, she's motioning me to come over ... I guess she's looking at me ... or else she's signalling to that trash can ... no, it's me. Better luck next time, Trash Can, that babe wants me, not you ... She's pointing to the empty seat beside her! I can do it ... come on, feet — first one foot, good, now the left — I'm doing it; I'm walking! Here I come, Kristy — not the hottest chick in the skillet, but I'm just an amateur — she'll do for target practice. She has the main qualification I require — she's *alive!* So, I'm following the yellow brick road to romance, and I've got my brain, my heart and my courage all under control, now back to my feet! I'm almost there ... yeah, I can woo this chick ... she'll think I'm Leonardo DiCaprio's twin. I'm cool — a Romeo in Reeboks! Oh, hi, Kristy ... sure, I've been wanting to talk to you, too ... nah, there's nothing wrong with my feet!

Graduation Jitters

Well, kid, you look pretty sharp in this cap and gown. I didn't say smart — you didn't make the Honor Society — but a B average senior year isn't so bad for a kid who was a Dodo Bird in second-grade reading groups — always wanted to be a Cardinal or a Blue Jay or even a Buzzard — always had trouble with my a-e-i-o-u's. I wish I had a few more months in high school — can't believe I'm saying that! — after all the griping I've done, all the classes I've skipped the past four years! Nobody can cut a class like this kid! But I'm just so confused now — can't decide what to do, and Dad's putting the pressure on me, "Get a full-time job, go to college or enlist!" He's not allowing any time off for good behavior ... not that I'd qualify! I really just wanted to hang out this summer and see what develops, but Pop's not buying that ... or a new car for me!

I've talked to counselors, taken aptitude tests up the kazoo — no money in trimming doggie toenails, and I'm too big to be a jockey! And Gram is cutting me out of the will if I don't go to college! So, what's left? My Uncle Don said he'd train me to be a butcher ... but to cut up little cows! I used to raise and name them in 4-H ... and they followed me around like puppies. Nah, I couldn't cut them into pieces!

Dad says I'm too stupid or lazy to be a lawyer ... Uncle Bob says those are two prerequisites to being a good lawyer! Grandpa says I can help him at the bakery, but who wants to get up at two a.m. to make donuts?

Nope, I've got to think of something ... quick! I tried for the old "let me go to Europe and discover myself" routine. Dad said, "Fine. You want to sail around the world — join the Navy!" Then, we'd be back to getting up early, being on task, boot camp or wherever sailor dudes go to! I want to do something relaxing. Dad says I get to relax when I'm 65 ... if I'm lucky and have a retirement plan, social security and no naggin' wife!

The counselor asked what I'd like to do. When I told him babe watchin', video games, football on TV, and polishing my car that didn't impress him much.

I've tried to explain to Dad that I'll "find myself" ... and soon. But I guess I'll be doing the finding at college. I don't want an eight to five job now ... maybe never! So, it looks like I'm back to the books. But everybody says college is lots easier than high school ... and I got through that pretty easy — learned to suck up to the teachers, made friends with all the brains, dated smart girls! Yep, I knew all the tricks! That's it ... I'll go to college, seek new opportunities, widen my horizons. I'll find a major that suits my talents — there's gotta be something out there for me. Yes, this cap and gown were made for me, Sam Hopkins, high school grad ... and scholar!

I'm a Stud

Do you know anyone who looks like Stallone? Do you know anyone who looks in the mirror, flexes, and the mirror says "Wow"? Do you know anyone who makes the gym equipment cry out in pain when he enters the Buff Body Builders? No? No? Then, you don't know *me!* I was born with Schwarzenegger-sized biceps! I crawled faster, walked sooner, threw my pacifier farther!

My dad's a lifter (weights, not shop!) and he's passed the dumbbell on to me. When other kids were ridin' trikes, throwin' Frisbees, teeter-totterin' ... I was pumpin' little bits of iron, liftin' mini-weights. While other kiddos were lickin' ice cream cones and wolfin' hot dogs ... I was being stuffed with body-buildin' whey, proteins, and weight gainers. Their rooms were filled with stuffed animals, toys, puzzles ... nothing soft in my room. All my so-called playthings were made of iron and steel! My walls were plastered with ribbons and certificates — reminders of the glory a body beautiful wins! Of course, in sports I'm unbeatable — Jordan before retirement ... Pete Rose without a bookie!

What's it like being a stud muffin? Well, I could stammer a little, be modest, but it's too late for that. I was born to be in the limelight ... to out-shine the moon ... to be a star! I don't need a phone booth to change into Superman! Little old ladies help *me* across the street! I make Stallone and Schwarzenegger look like mama's boys! I've already got agents knocking at my door, promising me one-way tickets to the big time! Am I interested in making it to the top? Do I want all the work I've put into this mountain of muscle to pay off? You betcha! I think I'll start with the NFL and work my way into sportscasting ... the movies ... watch out, Arnold!

My dad's behind me all the way (pushing ... pushing), but Mom wants me to get a degree. She says if I injure a knee it's all over, but they can't take a diploma away from me. We'll see ... I don't know how much time I'll have to study — with sports and all these women hangin' on my muscle-toned body! Oh, did I forget to mention that little tidbit? Chicks love a good bod. I know they like brains, too. My friend Sam writes love poems — they love that. Tim paints super pictures — makes girls smile. Stan's a mathematical genius, computer guru — girls flock to him when their brains hit a snag. But it's Muscle Boy who really turns them on. It's Macho Man they want to go out with! From kindergarten on, girls seemed to recognize or be drawn to my charisma, my powerfulness. Did I fight this gravity that brought me girl gifts? Heck, no! I lapped up the attention — considered it payback for all the hours making this he-man body.

So, where am I going now ... what's the plan? Well, I've been offered college scholarships to all the biggies. I'll choose one ... make Mom happy. Then, after I get a little smarts in my brain (the one muscle I haven't stretched and strained) I'll get on with my life — hopefully the lifestyle of the rich and famous! I want to see my image on posters, magazine covers, movie screens. Yep, I'm takin' this manly chest all the way! I'm destined for glory. I've been trained for it ... and I'm ready ... 'cause ya see, I'm a stud!

I'm Losing My Sex Appeal

Nah, it can't be true; I can't be losing that special something I've always had that attracted girls like school lunch attracts Alka Seltzer! I was born under a babe star — one look at my big baby blues and chicks were climbin' walls to get a look at Mr. Awesome. It started in the nursery at the hospital. The pink-blanketed ones cried till their beddies-on-wheels were placed closer to the hunk baby in blue! I got all the girls' graham crackers in kindergarten, and in the first grade even the teacher was in love with me! I won every election in grade school. Where there was a knock-kneed female with a voting crayon, I was a born winner! They did all my homework, ate my vegetables, brought me candy and fought off the bullies who called me "pretty-boy."

In middle school I was still a heart crusher. When I walked by uniformed, underdeveloped co-eds, the eyelids began to flutter like butterflies in a tornado. The newly-elected cheerleaders made up yells about me! Uncoordinated drill team squads only had eyes for me; squeaky-voiced glee club girls put my name in their "Hallelujah Chorus"! I was the most photographed guy in the yearbook — only girls are dedicated enough to stay after school to make a yearbook. The girls gave me a standing ovation when I played Romeo in the eighth-grade play, and they all snubbed the Juliet girl the rest of the year. Hell hath no fury like eighty girls belting out "Wherefore art thou, Romeo?" and seventy-nine being rejected!

But high school, now, is a different story. Oh, I took the school by storm my freshman year ... college-bound senior girls were writing sonnets about me, prom queens saved me a seat at the head lunch table, clueless sophomore girls gazed hungrily from the sidelines. But things started changing slightly my second year. I just barely won the Guy-to-Die-for contest. Kent Sharp was a close runner-up — I'd never had a runner-up before! I just wrote it off as a fluke ... computer error in counting the votes. Then, I knew the gods were turning against me when the results of the photography class's "Photo Face" ended in a tie! I ran to the mirror, mirror on the wall (which usually winked boldly at me) and said, "Is this the face that launched a thousand female phone calls?" Something was going on ... changing. I think it's my world as I know it! Could I possibly be losing my sex appeal? Is it like a deodorant stick — the thicker you lay it on, the faster you use it up? Is it like an Everready — needs frequent recharging? Will it lie dormant for a while ... like flowers ... and bloom again in the spring, brighter than ever? Did I burn it at both ends till it flickered out? I guess only time will tell ... "To be or not to be" ... with sex appeal, "that is the question!"

Issues

Teens are supposed to be strange. It's a mixed-up time of life. It's a proven fact during these years the brain is in reverse and the hormones are in full speed ahead! So, this being the case, why the big deal about teenage issues? For instance, this kid Jack really ... I mean, *really* likes hubcaps. He nails them to his walls, he flies them like a Frisbee, he *eats* out of one instead of a plate! He's a Hubcap Hypo! "Caps can be found everywhere," says Jack, "junk yards, garage sales, swap meets," ... and sometimes, I'm sorry to say, on parked cars!

Mario digs celebrities — he's a groupie for anyone who's had his name in print ... excluding the obituaries! He spends all of his money on stamps, writing for autographed pictures. He's had a little luck getting star shots: Robin Williams sent him some great prints, but most of the ones on his wall he cut from magazines and autographed himself!

Dana has more than a hundred bottles of nail polish — she does each nail (even toenails) with a different polish ... then she gives each a glittery overcoat. Steve has eight holes in each ear ... two in his nose ... and the old belly button's been drilled four times. OK, OK, some of these issues may appear a little deranged, but remember our grandmothers went round and round with a hula hoop!

My own thing is much more sensible ... more tame ... much more mature — I have a fetish for duct tape. You heard me, *duct tape!* I fell for my first roll when I was putting posters up in my room. Masking tape lost its hold, Scotch tape was a waste of time ... but duct tape had real holding power! I started using it on everything — to fix the chapped-lip upholstery on Dad's pick-up, to crisscross the lawn chairs, to add a decorative border to my room, and to put my little sister's Barbie's legs back on its dainty butt! I wear duct tape on the knees of my jeans to cover the worn-out spots. (A teenage guy does a lot of beggin' to get dates!) I wear T-shirts that say,"Stick it ... up... with duct tape!" I thought my mind would explode with ecstasy when I went to the city and discovered

33

the tape in designer colors — it was too much! My creative soul swung into action and a million new uses took shape. Dad finally brought me down from duct tape heaven by limiting me to five rolls of the colored wonder. I ask you, would they have limited Van Gogh to five colors … oops, maybe they did, he committed suicide! Would Michelangelo have finished the Sistine Chapel ceiling with five lousy colors?

I'm sure by now you've stamped me as a Twilight Zone escapee … well, you just don't know what a hold this stuff has on me. So, before you judge me, I want to say in my own defense I think the world would have been a better place if others before me had invested in a few rolls of the sticky stuff. For instance, the King's horses and all of his men could have used a few strips to put old Humpty Dumpty together again. I think the reason that wall in Berlin stood as long as it did was duct tape! Dorothy should have used it to mark her way back to Kansas. Chicken Little could have made sure the sky wasn't falling, and I've no doubt Jill could have patched Jack's broken crown if she'd carried a wad of this tape in her fanny bag.

So, now you know my little secret — I am stuck on duct tape and duct tape's stuck on me! And at this moment I've got one mega job for this super product — see if it can stand up to a real test! We'll see if it can hold together a broken heart — Adrianne just dumped me for a trombone player!

I've Got Gas!

It may not sound too exciting to most people — my new summer job pumpin' gas — but to me it's the perfect job. I know it's not glamorous like being a lifeguard at some swanky pool or beach, but it sure beats flippin' burgers. I don't get rich, but I make enough to keep me goin'. I also get discounts on my gas and car repairs. When you have a car as old as mine, that's worth a lot.

This may sound weird, but I like cleanin' windshields. I know I shouldn't enjoy scraping bug guts off glass, but there's a certain satisfaction to washing away travel grime. I like airing the tires and feeding hungry gas tanks. Now, I'll admit the customers are sometimes Twinkieville characters — I get a lot of old ladies, 'cause as you know: *Real* men pump their *own* gas! Now, I have nothing against these AARP centerfolds — in fact, they're my best patrons. But I do wish they could remember which side their tank's on, and how to open their hoods. These golden oldies always want their water and oil checked, but I have to help them out of their seats, so I can search for the hood release. And that's no easy task! The up-side, though, is I often get a good tip.

I also have a set of female regulars who don't qualify for Medicare. They're from the country club set … driving a Lexus or Mercedes … too rich to get gas on their manicured nails. They're much harder to please than the Geritol gals, and never tip as well. I'm really surprised they don't have chauffeurs doing their driving — they have the perfect stuck-up voices to say, "Home, James!"

Now, the *real* plus to my job is … once a week Adrianne Morain wheels into my station for a fill-up. Don't tell my boss, but I'd work here for free just for the chance to wipe Adrianne's windows, air her tires, gas her tank! Adrianne's the hottest number in school — way out of my class, but once a week I get to look and dream! She never looks at me or says my name … just, "Hey, you …" even though **Steve** in big, bold letters is printed on my shirt. She just gazes through me with her rich-girl eyes.

I think she smiled at me once, or maybe it was just a hiccup. Of course, she never pays — just waves her dainty little hand and says, "Charge it to Daddy!" I can't tell you what a thrill it is to have Adrianne spin out ... throwing gravel in my eyes and until next week's visit, leaving an empty space in my heart!

Now I guess you know why I like my job. Other guys may make more money ... have more challenging part-time careers ... but me ... well, I like what I do — I've got gas!

Lock Up

I don't know how lockers are assigned in your school, but in ours you get one when you're a freshman and keep it till you graduate. All the lockers are in a central area, and the classrooms take off in all directions. So, since your lock box belongs to you for four years, you become well-acquainted and attached to it.

Now, these tin vessels become our catch-alls ... our mini-home-away-from-home ... our trash collectors! And sometimes they house a few trinkets that we'd be ashamed to show our grannies or our Sunday school teachers. The librarian got quite a jolt going through my locker looking for a lost copy of *Tale of Two Cities*. She was pretty cool — gave me the evil eye and said, "You little Dickens!"

I sometimes think after four years our lockers take on personalities; I call mine Chuckie and I treat him right — feed him top quality stuff. Perry calls his Hefty and fills it full of nothing but trash. He really believes that Hefty devours it ... ya gotta know Perry! Cliff calls his Sex Machine — has it lined with good-looking women ... from magazines — Cliff's never spoken to a real girl! And across the hall from us is Becky Roger's locker ... old #428 — we named it Hot Lips. We're sure that steam comes out all four corners, and we're absolutely sure, beyond a reasonable doubt, that her combination is 36-24-37! We like to walk by and inhale the sweet scent of an untouchable dream — sure, Becky's off-limits to us, but we can sniff her locker whenever we want ... if no normal person's around!

Now, in a couple of weeks I have to think about leaving old Chuckie (and Hot Lips, too, of course) — no lockers in college. I really don't want to turn custody of old Chuck over to some snot-nosed freshman; we've been through too much together. He's shared my smiles and laughter when everything was going my way, and took a couple of punches (sorry, fella) when the world turned upside-down! Oh sure, I'll come back and visit ... but without my beat-up notebooks, dirty sweat socks, unfinished assignments, Chuckie'll take on a new life. There's a nasty rumor that all the lockers are going to be painted red — not a good Chuckie color! But perhaps it's just idle custodial gossip! But no matter what, I'm going to have to put old #416 up for adoption. It's for his own good. I couldn't ask them to retire it like a famous athlete's number! No, I'll just walk away from the best locker ever ... without tears. I'll walk away and not look back at my old friend ... but I'll always remember that he was one Tin Man who already had a heart!

Makin' Me a Man

For some reason my dad decided I needed to be toughened up! He didn't come right out and say, "Son, you're a wimp, a 'fraidy cat, a shrimp," but I could see the question in his eyes when I played my violin instead of playing linebacker on the football team. So began the "make a man of Brian" campaign. I shook with fear when I saw Dad filling up the garage with sports gear — fishing tackle, camping equipment, weights and sports paraphernalia. I begged Mom to stand between me and this determined look in Dad's eye! She just laughed and said he was really doing it for himself; he needed to get in touch with his inner sporting-self, and he was taking me on the journey with him!

We started our new male bonding with memberships in a gym — we lifted, pumped, stretched and strained till Dad developed a hernia ... a lucky break for my achin' back. After he healed from his surgery, we went camping in the Colorado mountains — a surefire manly escapade! I wouldn't say it was a wasted experience, but poison ivy, a leaky tent, getting lost and being chased by a bear probably contributed to Dad's insane laughter as he happily burned the tent in our backyard.

After Dad's eyebrows grew back, and because he's one of those get-back-on-the-horse guys, Dad bought a fishing boat and rented a cabin on the lake. He invested in rods and reels and every kind of fishing lure. Dad never does anything moderately — he even insisted I wear one of those floppy, old-man, fishing hats! I must admit we came home with frozen fish ... plus stitches in Dad's neck where his hook made a big catch ... and strep throat which got its start when Dad dropped his rod and reel into the drink and thought his hip boots would be high enough for the retrieve! "We'll get our fish from the supermarket from now on," were Dad's last words as he gave his fishing gear to the Salvation Army.

Because he doesn't give up easily, and because he hoped spectator sports would take less penicillin, Dad and I started attending sports events. We hit a lot of baseball games. (I liked the billboards and Dad got

hit by a foul ball.) The Lakers came to town. (I loved the music at half-
time; Dad tripped going down the bleachers and twisted his left ankle.)
For my birthday we drove out to see the Broncos. (I got a football jersey
and hat; Dad got a new car ... his BMW didn't do well on the snow-
packed Colorado roads!)

Finally Dad has lost interest, heart and enthusiasm for sports and
male bonding. He turns off the TV when a basketball game comes on,
and he hates the Broncos! He's cleaned all of the sports stuff out of the
garage. I think it's safe to say Dad's given up on "macho-fyin'" his son.
He's decided it's too hard on him to try to make a man out of me!

Mama's Boy, You Bet!

"You're a mama's boy," are fighting words to most guys. Yeah, hardly anybody wants to be accused of being a sissy — a kid overly protected by his mother. But you know something, I don't mind one bit. I get called that a lot ... I just grin and say, "Me? You got it — I'm the World's Biggest Mama's Boy!"

Lots of factors went into making me a Mom's kid. First and probably most important, I was the baby, and my mom really bit into that old "baby your baby" idea. My brothers and sisters were at least twelve years older. I think I was Mom's last grab at youth, or else as my sister Nikki says, "You were nothing but an unlucky accident!" Either way, I came out ahead, 'cause Mom has nurtured and babied me since the doctor gave me that first swat. (Incidentally, nobody's smacked my butt since ... Mama saw to that!) That's another thing about having an Angel of Mercy hanging over my shoulder: she never lets anybody hurt me! My brothers knew I was off-limits — nobody wanted to risk Momsy's wrath! The neighborhood bully only bothered me once; Mom made swift work of him. He still has scars and a higher pitched voice! I was saved from all sorts of situations during my school years. Mom took on teachers who wanted to discipline me; school lunch ladies who now fix meatloaf the way I like it; principals who *thought* they wanted to keep me after school — till they met Super Mom, and school board members who have added photography and championship chess to the curriculum to keep Mom from running for a school board position!

This sweet mother adjusts her life around mine. She takes off early every Thursday to see my games. She gets up early every morning to fix homemade biscuits just the way I like them — by the dozens! She makes sure my clothes are ready, my shoes shined and on occasion has done a little of my homework when I was in a bind. She got me a car, my own TV, a computer with all the games and my own phone line. I know this makes me sound like a spoiled brat — what can I say?

41

"What about your father," you ask, "didn't he try to straighten you out?" Well, Dad was older even than mom. He'd gone the distance on my brothers and sisters when he was in his prime. But now he has a remote and a rocking chair with his name on it, and in his semi-retirement voice he'll often yell, "Gladys, you're spoilin' the heck outta that kid!" But he's too tired to fight Gung-ho Gladys and her mighty motherhood campaign. My brothers and sisters just watch in amazement; it seems they were raised in the "spare the rod, spoil the child" era. They can't believe their once strict and now menopausal mother is letting their kid brother become the World's Number One Most Spoiled Jerk!

Will I outgrow this Mama-itis you ask? Do I want to? Well, I suppose someday I'll want to get married, but the girl will have to eat Kryptonite for breakfast to measure up to my Mommy! I haven't seen any yet who could pass the test; so, until that special someone comes along who'll grant my every wish, fill my every expectation, I'll just keep things like they are. Yep, I'll just relax ... kick back and enjoy being a Mama's Boy!

Mr. Perfect

Kip is a saint ... a shining example of everything that's perfect ... a role model for the world — especially me! You've guessed it, Kippie Boy's my older brother ... my perfect older brother. If you don't believe me, just ask my mother, my father, my grandparents, all the teachers in our school system, or the doctor who made his spectacular delivery! Yes, the universe may be at odds with itself about some things, but everybody's in agreement about the perfection of Kip. Now, I'm not saying some of these things aren't true — as brothers go, he's OK. I don't think he's a candidate for sainthood. (But I'm sure Mom's already made his reservation!) I don't, on the other hand, see him on the wide road to hell! He's got a few flaws, but the folks, even with x-ray glasses, wouldn't detect them.

I read once, and my own experience proves it to be true, that the first born gets the best from the old gene pool — the biggest shot of brain power, best of the family looks, sparkling personality! By the time the next kid rolls along, the good stuff's pretty much used up — leaving a lot of ordinary people! Now in some ways Kip and I are alike — we both have brown hair (His just happens to do that Tom Cruise thing); we both have above average intelligence (guess whose I.Q. is higher?); we both like good looking chicks (which one do you think the chicks like back?); we both love the computer. (He's looking up impressive facts to regurgitate at the dinner table, while I'm knee-deep in kiddie games!)

It's hard at home with the folks pointing out my failures ... and Kip's How-Great-Thou-Art successes! But it's much worse at school. In grammar school the teacher would start the year with, "Oh, you're Kip's brother," and end it with "You're Kip's brother?" In middle school the teacher expected the same — great artwork, honor roll, star athlete, great drummer! But instead they got a kid who couldn't draw a straight line with a ruler; average student; bench warmer, and rhythmless band drop-out! High school was a little better — I got into drama and debate and since those teachers didn't know "Kip the Flawless," I did OK. I even did a little wrestling ... a sport too lowly for Mighty Brother! I'm really enjoying my senior year. Mr. Wonderful's off to conquer new horizons at the university ... letting his light shine there instead of in my eyes! Yes, I can certainly say it hasn't been easy following in his footsteps. I suppose we'll become friends when we get old and bald. And if someday he'd need a kidney ... well, I'm not sure I'd give it to him, but it'd be nice to be asked! But for now I feel like I'm runner-up ... second string ... invisible ... standing in the shadow of my big brother Kip — Mr. Perfect!

My Imaginary Friend, Mr. Musclebutt

Go ahead and laugh. I'm a healthy sixteen-year-old male with an imaginary friend! I know I should have outgrown him with all my other childhood thingamabobs, but I didn't. I let them rip my blankie from my eight-year-old clutches, gave up G.I. Joe, donated my electric train to the Salvation Army, and sold my kiddie games at Mom's garage sale, but I kept Mr. Musclebutt! So, say it ... I'm a milksop, a wimp, a mama's boy ... but nothing you say will make me part with my imaginary friend. Have I taken lots of razzing about this friend? Yes! Marty says if I'm gonna have this phantom friend, at least it should be a hot chick. Have I embarrassed myself and family over this little obsession? Yes! When I insist on an extra place setting at the table, family eyes roll in unison! Have I been recommended for therapy? Yes! Mom has me on Charter's hotline! But all the controversy just makes Mr. Musclebutt more important in my life!

I met my special friend when I was four years old. It's really Gramps' fault. He took me to a wrestling match and Mr. Musclebutt followed me home. Mom said a puppy would have been easier to explain to the neighbors, her bridge club, the minister. (I wanted to have Musclebutt baptized!) What's so unique about this imaginary person, you ask? Well, for one thing, he's big and muscular ... he encourages me to work out. And I must say I'm pretty buff! He knows all about women and has helped me a lot with the babes. He has a sense of humor ... his jokes could be sent to Letterman. And man, can this guy keep a secret — he's shared all of my triumphs and defeats ... and never breathed a word. There's a lot to be said for having a friend that can only be seen and heard by you!

Now don't get me wrong, Mr. Musclebutt's not perfect. This figment of my imagination has an irritating problem — he *must* watch all the wrestling on TV. I had to get a part-time job to pay for the satellite dish so he wouldn't miss the Undertaker do his Tombstone move. My eyes are bloodshot from watching Mankind, Stone Cold, the Federation and, of course, his favorite — The Rock! My body parts hurt from practicing and mastering moves like the stunner and corporate elbow! The weird thing is, I don't really like wrestling — but don't tell Mr. Musclebutt, he'd put me in such a headlock ... my neck would snap, crackle and pop!

So, there you have it — I'm strange. When will I say, "See ya," to Mr. Musclebutt, you ask? I really can't say. It could be that I'll feel uncomfortable packing him off to college ... he might not be fraternity material! I can't see him joining the Marines with me — they only need a *few* good men! And I suppose when I marry, my bride might get a little huffy sharing our honeymoon with a 300-pound, tattooed wrestler! So, someday I'll have to make some serious decisions ... but till that day comes, I'm just layin' back, hangin' out, bein' cool with my main imaginary man — Mr. Musclebutt!

Nerd Herd

Yes, "Nerd Herd" ... that's what they call my friends and me. Does it hurt? Not much, nerd is just a four-letter word like *jock*! So what if we use correct grammar, always have our assignments done on time, understand higher math, know we'll actually use geometry one day, help the teachers with their limited computer skills. Sure, a couple of us wear the famous geek glasses, and Greg makes that snorty sound when he laughs, and we all bought suspenders to make a statement — we're nerds ... *deal* with it!

We weren't always different; we functioned normally in grade school. I guess we began to cluster together in junior high. Everybody looked at us differently when we could actually diagram sentences, liked reading library books, did extra science projects because we were hooked! We were never chosen for athletic teams, but everybody wanted to be our lab partners and computer buddies. We weren't ugly, nor were we outcasts; we were just smart guys marchin' to our own CD-ROM! We were invited to parties ... were very popular when Trivial Pursuit was the entertainment but not when they started playing kissy spin-the-bottle type games ... we're slow spinners!

We all found our niches in high school. Greg fit right in with the dramatic club ... always the ham and now has a place to channel that talent. Warren and his French horn made the music department wake up and pay attention. Scott's the number one man in Quiz Bowl ... has his valedictorian speech already written. I've made my mark as assistant editor on the *(Insert name of school paper)*. But we're still not school leaders; we're not "Who's Who" material; we're not members of the in-crowd. But we've all racked up good academic scholarships ... we've got a future! We'll become contributing citizens. And when we have our ten-year reunion ... who knows ... maybe like in an old movie, one of us will come back in a limo and sweep Kayla Winston, campus queen, off her feet! But, of course, no matter how successful we are, no matter what we accomplish, we'll always be remembered by our high school classmates as the Nerd Herd!

47

Planning Mr. Teufel's Retirement Party

It's sort of a tradition at our school for the students to plan retirement parties for the departing teachers. Now, there are some we're glad to see go. (We make their farewells quick and painless!) And then there are those who leave empty, hollow spaces in our hearts and hallways. This is how it'll be when we lose Mr. (Butch) Teufel — he's a great guy, a super shop teacher — a friend. He's never too busy to listen to our problems and always has time to crack a few jokes. And can that man work with wood! I hear he's single-handedly going to build a retirement home at Grand Lake, Colorado — and you can bet it'll be some showplace, too! The cabinets in our shop are hand-carved by this craftsman — he's a perfectionist ... plus! His wife might get ticked off by this "Mr. Perfect" trait, but we like it 'cause our shop projects come out top notch! So, the old boy deserves a good send-off!

We've had some real success stories in our day with these faculty farewells. A few years ago we had a blast — Mr. Evan's birthday was on the Fourth of July, so we decided on a fireworks theme. We had red, white and blue balloons, star-shaped cookies, red punch, and of course, a few firecrackers! OK, OK, things got out of hand ... but Workman's Comp paid for Mr. Evan's trip to the emergency room ... and his beard *finally* grew back!

Mr. Belteau always played Santa for our Christmas assemblies ... so, we went with a Yuletide party for his big send-off. He was delighted with the elves, packages and Christmas lights. He was a little gruff about the reindeer tracks and droppings in his office! Mrs. Filbert and Mrs. Carter took early retirement last year; they wanted to quit while they were still functioning mentally. (That being the case, Carter should have bowed out ten years ago!) Because Filbert's a part-time cosmetologist/teacher and Carter's a P.E. teacher/health nut, we planned a "healthy bad-hair day" with droopy tangled tresses. We all ate granola and wore ugly jogging suits!

But now the question's "What to do for Mr. Teufel?" Paul suggested a sleazy woman jumping out of a cake ... but at *his* age Teufel'd probably be more interested in the cake! I think we've pretty much decided on a fish-out! Butchie Boy loves to sail out in his little boat and fish for the big ones! We'll all wear those stupid hats decorated with hooks and lures ... and clomp around in hip boots! We've got a horse tank coming and a truckload of fishies. We'll plunk Teufel into an *easy* chair, hand him a cane pole and let him go fishing! Yep, that'll do it — a super way to give our friend Butch the heave-ho ... and what a way to go!

Shapin' Up

Herbie and I are gonna do it; we've been talking about it for years and now we're gonna put our money (we finally got some) where our mouths are — we're joining a gym! We're tired of being runts, ninety-pound weaklings with baby fat. We're gonna lift and pump till we're Schwarzenegger look-alikes. We'll be so buff mirrors will weep when we walk away! We'll have to special order T-shirts to go over our bulging biceps.

We would have made this move sooner, but we had to make some dough for the membership fee. We worked our butts off — painted fences, shoveled snow, mowed lawns and washed cars. But we've got the cash and are ready to become stud machines. I know, I know, it won't happen overnight. My brother warned us that we'd be sore and whine like mama's boys the first week. That's OK, 'cause we're tough and we'll hang in there — we'll sweat like pigs and smell like he-men! When we go back to school in the fall, we'll make everyone take a second look. Those bullies who pushed us around, threw our underwear in the shower and stuffed us in lockers better watch out. We're gonna be revenge-seeking Rambos on the rampage! (A good title ... might send it to Stallone.) So as you can see, this new tough guy image was a big motivator in our muscle-building campaign, but it wasn't the big reason for our macho makeovers. What's the one single thing (besides football and cars) that's in every thought a teenage guy has? What stirs his brain waves and charges his hormones? You've got it — Women! We did it for the babes! We want to get chicks; we want to have our pick instead of taking football players' leftovers. We want the first string — the rah-rah girls, the drill team leaders, the short-skirted baton twirlers! We're tired of settling for the drab doofus book-stackers in the library.

Girls will follow us around hoping for a chance to please the rugged rascals they used to taunt and ignore. But big-hearted, robust fellows that we'll be, we won't hold a grudge — there'll be plenty of us to go around.

50

The babes will be drawing straws to see who carries our books. It'll be great to be King!

Yep, we'll start slow, but because we're so determined we'll soon be benchin' 395 and squattin' 490 pounds. Our once spindly legs will be solid rocks; we'll have buns of aluminum! Our upper bodies will make our enemies envious — we'll be feared and admired by the masses. I can't wait for tomorrow to get here — it's the first day of the rest of our power-packed lives!

Sure Winner

I know my chances are better for getting hit by lightning. I know I stand a better chance of Cindi Morgan dating me or even looking at me. I know I stand a better chance of passing trig ... but there's just this gut feeling I have that someday I'll win the lottery!

I'm not going to just sit around and do nothing till this grand event occurs; I'll go ahead with my education — if I can wheedle, beg or get some sort of miracle tutoring that will get me through trigonometry, that is. But I won't sweat it — 'cause I know I have this little Lotto Fairy sitting on my shoulder waiting to spit the winning numbers in my ear!

I was just a punk kid when I first started watching ... every Saturday night ... those little numbered ping-pong balls being sucked out of that big jar! I'd see Mom frantically writing them and Dad pulling his weekly chances from his worn, tattered billfold. They never won anything, but Dad's poor-sport, losing outbursts sure enriched my vocabulary! I was fascinated by the whole process — the numbers, the balls, the money! I was six when I looked at my folks after a bad losing streak and said, "Don't worry, when I'm old enough to buy my own ticket, I'm gonna win this silly old lottery!" And I still believe this — I was born to win!

It's true I haven't won much else in my seventeen years — didn't win the free throw tournament; lost out to Buzz Kerns when they picked quarterback; missed the boat when Honor Society was announced; didn't stand a chance of being class officer; spelling bees were never my thing; didn't even try out for student council; Prom King, school newspaper editor, Most-likely-to-succeed title — all racked up in my lifelong losing streak! But am I depressed? Do I curse the fates or bang my head against a fence post? Do I run to Mommy like a slobbering crybaby? Well, ... Mom is a good listener ... has soft shoulders ... hmmm. But no, I pull myself up to my full 5'6" and laugh in the face of defeat — because I know someday none of those contests will matter! Right, when I cash in *big* I'll never count my losses!

And the good news is — I'll share my long-awaited riches! My folks will be showered with gifts —starting with a new wallet for Dad. I'll donate to charities and churches. I'll build the school a new football stadium and buy the teachers all the chalk they want! I won't hold grudges; I'll be the most Scroogeless winner in lottery history. And maybe, just maybe, with big piles of hundred dollar bills piled around me, Cindi Morgan will actually look at me! Wow! Now you know … that someday … some place when I least expect it, I'll smile … 'cause I just won the lottery!

To Tell or Not to Tell

I've got to decide ... quick. My friend, Barkley, has a gun in his locker! I don't know how he got in the school with it, but I do know why. He's tired of all the kids picking on him; he's little and scrawny — always been an easy target for the jocks. He said he's tired of it ... he's going to show them! I tried to get him to put the gun in my gym bag and take it out to my car. But he wouldn't do it. I don't really think he'll use it. He just wants it as a threat to make his tormentors back off. He promised to take it home tonight ... and he swears he doesn't even have any bullets. Since I know, I'll be in trouble if I don't squeal. I suppose I better tell Mr. Sparks, the vice principal, he's a good guy. But if I turn Barkley in, he'll be suspended for the rest of the year! His dad would kill him ... his grades are shaky already ... he wouldn't graduate.

Oh, I don't know what's the right thing to do. I wish he hadn't told me. I'm his best friend, but I don't need to know everything ... especially something like this! Maybe I should ask Miss Carter, that counselor Barkley likes ... She's been working with him since I told her some of his problems. I thought she was making some headway ... till now! I don't know why some kids have to pick on other kids ... Some just need a scapegoat. They're so insecure on the inside, the only way they feel good about themselves is when they're putting someone else down. And the victim is usually some defenseless person like Barkley. And years of this harassment will sometimes drive even the strongest kid over the edge. The newspapers are full of cases of kids killing kids.

I've always been worried that Barkley spends so much time at his video games. He's fascinated with the violence — his favorites are rated "mature" which is like an R rating for a movie. I like some of the games myself, but all that emphasis on guns and blood ... and now Barkley has a gun in his locker!

That does it, I'm getting a pass to see Miss Carter. I couldn't live with myself if something happened and I was too big a wimp to stop it. She'll know what to do. She'll take care of the situation and try to help Barkley too. I'll feel like a snitch, but that's better than being a witness. Well, here I go ... Barkley will probably never speak to me again, but it's the right decision ... it's the only decision.

What's that noise? Oh, no, it's the crisis alarm! Mr. Hatfield has locked the door ... He's making us get against the back wall, away from all the windows. He'll never give me a pass to the counselor now. Let's see, crisis alert ... oh no, it says here in my school agenda "crisis alarm may mean an intruder in the building ... often armed!" Please don't let it be Barkley ... let me not be too late to help my friend ... Oh, God, let it just be a practice drill!

TV Addicts

It's not true — I'm *not* addicted to television. I'm *not* hooked on the boob tube. I don't lose my balance and break into cold sweats whenever the remote's out of my grubby little hand! OK, I'll admit I *like* a little TV, but who doesn't? My minister mentioned *Everybody Loves Raymond* in last week's sermon ... and it's not even G-rated! My old English teacher, Ms. Pureheart, watches Oprah and Letterman, and she's a Shakespeare freak! Why, Mom's bridge club spends most of their time discussing all the evil that takes place in their daytime soaps. Even my old Granny plants herself in front of her fifty-four inch Sony to see *Golden Girl* reruns and do a little swingin' and swayin' with some old geezer called Lawrence Welk! So, see ... I'm not some oddball goon because I spend a few minutes a day eyeballing the old television set!

The fact that I own my own TV set (with a VCR) doesn't prove a thing. Santa brought them last Christmas 'cause I'd been more nice than naughty! But I don't watch this magic box all the time; I'm a student — I attend high school; I have a life for cripes' sake! Sure, the minute I hit the house I take cover in my room, and I often flip the switch. MTV does fill a certain void in my life while I'm having an after-school snack and doing a little homework!

I will say this in my defense — I *never* watch the news or any of those *Dateline, 60 Minutes, 48 Hours* type shows, so there must be some hope for me! I take a peek when the folks are watching *Wheel of Fortune*. I don't know if it's the challenge I like or Vanna's wardrobe! I know you're going to find out anyway, so I'll confess I never miss a few shows like *Baywatch* and *South Park*, *(Current popular shows may be substituted as appropriate)* and I'm really partial to some of the movie channels. OK, on the occasional Saturday morning you *could* catch me scoping the cartoons as I spoon down a couple bowls of Fruit Loops! And since I know the polygraph test is next, I'll just go ahead and spell it out — W. W. F. — I'm really sold on wrestling ... the thrill of the ring ... the showmanship... the *pain!* What teenager could resist this kind of entertainment? Not me ... so, there you have it! I'm a TV junkie; perhaps I'll give it up someday ... go cold turkey. Maybe I need help; I hear there's a good shrink on FOX at 8:30 — maybe I'll tune him in tonight as I'm flipping through the channels!

Wanna Be a Kid Again

Everybody's always said to me, "Grow up, grow up, grow up!" Well, they were wrong ... they should have let me be a kid as long as possible! Now hear this, world, I don't want to grow up! It looks to me like kids have it made — no taxes, no bills, no divorces, no bankruptcy, no insurance, no politics, no job stress, no stock crashes, no alimony! Now why, I ask you, would I want to take on all those problems and give up the good stuff — ice cream, bicycles, long summers, swimming, toys. Yep, I think I'd rather go back instead of going forward! Where's a good time machine when you need it?

I think an eight or nine year old has it made. He only has to worry about long division and cleaning behind his ears once a week! He hasn't discovered the opposite sex, so that's one less hassle! He can read comics, play video games, scope out the Net, go fishin' with Grandpa and eat peanut butter from the jar! He just needs one best friend and a good dog. He still wants to believe in Santa Claus, the Easter Bunny and the Tooth Fairy. He lives on his allowance, catches fireflies on a summer night, likes to wrestle and tell tall tales. Life's simple ... life's good!

And now that I'm eighteen — graduating from high school in two days, standing on the threshold of adulthood — now that I see all the responsibility I'm soon to face, it scares the heck out of me! I want to crawl back into that safety zone ... that time of nursery rhymes and recess! But one can't go backwards — must go full speed ahead, take the plunge, never look back, take no prisoners, be a *Man!*

So, I'm going out there — leaving all my toys and security blankets behind. I'm going to take this giant leap for mankind hoping that the world is fair, and with the right attitude and hard work anything's possible. I've watched others take this journey and fail ... or at least trip and come out bruised and disillusioned. I'll admit I'm a little shaky ... feeling naked in a roomful of flash cameras! But a man's gotta do ... So, I'll do it ... *tomorrow!* I've still got two days ... so, I'm gonna get my skateboard, grab a Snickers, put on my headphones and head for the beach. I'll be a man tomorrow ... but today, for a few more hours, *I'm gonna be a kid again!*

Wanna Bet?

I guess I have a bad habit. No, I don't bite my grubby fingernails; nah, I don't scratch myself in public; no way do I chew Red Man. (I like my gums too much!) No, my one weakness, my fatal flaw, my Achilles' heel — I like to gamble! No, I don't fly to Las Vegas for weekend jaunts — I'm only seventeen for Pete's sake! I'm not talkin' mob gamblin'; I don't place bets with a bookie — I just like to make a little wager on stuff.

When I was a kid I always bet with marbles: "Betcha I can shoot this cat's eye farther than you ... 'cause my G. I. Joe needs a new pair of shoes!" Then, I graduated to money: "Bet a nickel I can swing higher ... run faster ... yell louder!" My mom tried to put a stop to my obsessive behavior by taking a dime from my bank every time she heard me make a bet. This creative parental punishment put a halt to my wagering for a spell ... but one day I found myself betting myself on how long I'd wait till I started betting again!

My habit really bloomed in junior high; you can get some awesome bets going in that Never-Never-Land arena: "Betcha a hot roll you can't keep that casserole surprise down." ... "Betcha I'm on a roll and get more detentions this quarter than anyone in our class." ... "Betcha my losing-streak butt stays on the bench more than any other fearless Bulldog." ... "Betcha I cash out and my parent/teacher conferences set a Guiness record!"

But, of course, high school was the best backdrop for my gambling game! My bogus buddies and I discovered chicks (Yeah, it's true the other guys knew about them in fifth grade.) and a whole new gaming board opened up. With the help of my user-friendly computer, graphs and colorful charts added to this game. I sold chances on my pick-a-loser board — the winner being the poor schmuck with the lowest dating score. My masterpiece scheme was the trashman lottery. No, it's not some fly-by-night crap shoot — the bets were on what lady killer would be dumped more often than the garbage! It was all in fun ... and Cory was thrilled to get the attention ... and those betting on him pocketed some big dough!

I also organized football pots, basketball kitties, baseball odds and the ever-popular Blank Diploma Pot — cash collectors were those picking the graduates whose diplomas would be as bare as a newborn baby's butt.

I guess I could stop this fascination I have with numbers, pots, odds, etc., but why should I? My minister and therapist suggest I abstain, go cold turkey, cash in my chips, kiss Lady Luck good-bye. I know my mom would be relieved. And who knows, maybe I will ... or maybe I won't ... what do you think? Want to hazard a guess? Want to lay even money? Wanna make a bet?

What a Sport

Sports — that's what it's all about. Fancy cars don't turn me on (even though a guy needs wheels). I don't give a spit about video games ... and movies for the most part are a bore (Unless Harrison Ford or some beautiful chicks are in it). Now don't get me wrong, I do like girls, but if I had to choose between a babe and the NFL ... there's no contest! 'Cause, you see, with females — who, by the way, will try to flirt their way into your sports-ridden mind — you don't have the competition, the brute strength, the intense action. (It takes months of constant attention and gift-giving to get *any* action from a girl!)

From the time I got my first basketball rattle, wore football-printed diapers, had a pacifier shaped like a baseball, I knew I was going to be a super sports fan! My dad and grandpa led the parade that shaped me into the athletic nut you see today. Grandpa has season tickets to the Bulls' games, so Dad and I are frequent fliers to Chicago. I'm never separated from my Bulls jacket, and my most prized possession is my autographed Jordan poster! Dad, on the other hand, is a football fanatic — he worships at the cleated feet of the Cowboys. (I like their cheerleaders myself, 'cause I'm a Colts man.) But I'll watch anything that wears helmets and struggles with pigskin. Baseball's not my favorite, but whenever the Yankees are playin', I'm watchin'! It doesn't take much to get me to watch a good hockey game, a wrestling match (Staged or not, it's quite a show.) or a round of golf — besides my prized poster, thanks to Uncle Mac, I have autographed pictures of Arnie Palmer and Jack Nicklaus. So, you see, I'm a well-rounded sports enthusiast.

In my athletic-crazed life I'm not just a spectator. I've worn the school colors in the football stadium, on the basketball court and on the baseball field. Because I've scored for the team, I've scored with the chicks. I don't get this — a letter jacket turns on the babes like Vegas neon. They hate the plays, but love the players; they just go to a game to gossip — see who's with who and eat hot dogs! They don't know an end zone from a no parking zone! But they'll do whatever it takes to date the jock who catches the most passes, scores the most baskets, hits the most home runs. But if you ask a female to stay home to watch the play-offs instead of seeing a Brad Pitt movie, you'd think you asked her to pass out raisins in an alligator pit.

Perhaps someday I'll outgrow this serious addiction ... but I doubt it. Dad and Grandpa are still going strong — sportswise! Maybe someday I'll give up the crowds, the scoreboard, the excitement of sports ... but for now just give me a big screen TV, plenty of sub sandwiches and a cold one (if Mom's not around) and I'm a happy man!

Girls

Babysitting Blues

There's got to be an easier way for a girl to make a living than taking care of somebody's bratty kids! My dad won't let me be a car hop at Sonic. Mom doesn't like the hours at the few shops in the mall who hire teenagers. She says I'll neglect my studies. She thinks it's a snap doing homework while Willie's clogging the toilet with his mommy's pantyhose, and little Rachel has been in the makeup again and looks like Bozo the Clown! Kids just aren't the same as they were when Mom babysat. "Just be firm and take lots of treats in your purse for bribes," comes the motherly advice as I head off for another night of babysitter's hell!

The delinquents *du jour* have magic kits they use to sabotage me the minute the folks leave the driveway. The father, by the way, is a warden in our state prison. I've searched the house thoroughly for handcuffs. At some point in their lives, I predict that this father and son will do mucho bonding at the state's expense! The real kicker is how Mrs. Warden always says, "You won't have anybody over, will you?" She's sure safe on that one — I don't know anyone with a protective vest and a machine gun! Any guy who might possibly think of dating me isn't strong enough to manipulate these kids — he'd for sure get hurt, be a starter on the football team, and I'd be on the coach's hit list!

Besides what babysitting does to my nerves and psyche, think how it's killing my social life! I'd love to be making lifetime connections at the Burger Hut. I could be studying dance or drama — taking that first step toward fame and fortune. I could be draggin' the boulevard, scoping out the guys! But noooo — the only guys I see are wearing Pampers and sucking pacifiers! So, thanks to my need for financial security, I'll probably be a social reject, a wallflower with babysitting references — never asked to pledge a sorority, left to be an old maid withering on the vine. (Not that I ever want to have children — not after what I've seen!)

I really think if people are going to have kids they should stay home with them — not push them off on money-hungry teenagers with poor combat skills. I think they should have to sign an agreement at the hospital promising never to abandon the little hellions, even for an evening, till they're eighteen years old. Maybe they could have one night off a year for good behavior *if* they have a Granny who is a trained wrestler. I know this would put me out of a job ... but it might also save my popularity, my self-esteem, my sanity!

I think it's time that we babysitters of America say "Whoa! We've had it! You had these kids ... you raise them!" Let's form a pact, girls, go on strike! They can't pay us enough to compensate for their child-rearing failures. Are you with me, Sister Sufferers? From now on, when they call for relief, for a night out away from little Dennis the Menace ... just say no!

Best Friends

Webster's says a friend is "a person attached to another by respect or affection," and there are so many quotes, poems, songs and one of TV's best sitcoms is called *Friends!* And who wouldn't want to be real friendly with Matthew Perry? And have you ever noticed how many greeting cards are female friend-to-friend? So, Hallmark knows there's something marketable in this friend business. And, you know, I've always admired those girls who have *"best friends."* You see them wearing matching shirts, sharing their Twix bars, being locker-mates. Well, having a best friend just doesn't work for me because, you see, I could never find one person who fits all of my requirements. This doesn't make me unfriendly, it's just that I have different needs for different deeds!

For instance, I call Kathy when I'm feeling down, when my latest hot romance has turned to cold potatoes. She's always cheery and can help me concentrate on the positive — my looks, my great personality, my outstanding wit ... OK, she's a little bit of a suck-up, but sometimes we all need to have our good qualities exaggerated! If nothing else, Kathy tells how her own love life is in the toilet, too! By the time I hang up, I'm feeling better — ready to get back on that dating horse and give cupid another chance to put one of his poisoned little darts right through my heart!

Now when I'm feeling flirty and full of adventure, I swing by Abby's place. Yes, Abby's the party-girl type. She has every eligible guy's number committed to memory, and if there's anything happening you can bet Abby knows about it. If nothing's going on, Abby can stir something up in minutes. Some of my best groundings have come after an Abby outing.

When it's getting close to finals, I become very chummy with Lisa. She's so smart the teachers are afraid of her — nobody likes to be intellectually put down in her own classroom. She's a walking encyclopedia ... not a recommendation that guys are looking for on weekend dates — unless their term paper is due on Monday! I can catch up on all the classes I've skipped in a matter of minutes when Lisa turns on her brain beacon. I sure hope I don't have to tag along behind her at college catching educational scraps ... it'll really cramp my style — she wants to be a mortician!

When I'm in the mood for a good old gossip session, I join Julie at the Hamburger Hideout. In the time it takes to order, eat and digest a double deluxe, I'm caught up on the whos, whats, whys, wheres and way-to-gos of everybody's love life! The way this girl sucks up dirt, her middle name should be Kirby!

Occasionally, I want to go to a sad show and cry a bucket of tears — it's good for the soul — a little hard on the makeup! Tess is my choice in sharing the old box of Kleenex ... she uses up half a box during the coming attraction. Nobody has such active tear ducts as this sob sister. It's true we both go home emotionally wrung out after one of these tear-jerkers, but what teenage girl can resist a movie that provides enough waterworks to wash the popcorn salt off her chin?

So you see where I'm going? Why it would be impossible for me to ever have a best friend? I need a battalion of them ... one just won't do ... like right now I'm looking for someone who'll make me laugh. I read if you have a friend who makes you laugh, you should pay them because every chuckle prolongs your life by days. So, I'm in the market for a laugh-a-minute friend! Do you know somebody who'd like to fill out an application? Are there any teenage Roseannes out there? Well, I'm off now ... on a quest ... I'll find her — somebody who'll tickle my funny bone ... a new buddy who'll say comical lines — and give me laugh lines — another pal, a funny one!

Bookworm

I am helplessly and totally addicted to books. I like the looks, the shapes, the smell of books. I have my room papered in book jackets. I know you can't judge a book by its cover, but some sure make a good pattern on the wall! I still have my Dr. Seuss books — mint condition! My end tables are stacks of books! I have to wear sunglasses to school because my eyes are so bloodshot from reading, and nothing "gets the red out" of these bookworm blinkers! What can I say, I'm a book junkie!

I must confess I'm not quite as sentimental over textbooks, although, I do have a slight crush on a couple of my literature texts. My name is on the Do Not Admit list posted at both school and public libraries. I just go wild in there — so many entrancing volumes from which to choose. But that's not my problem with the library officials — it's not the getting of the books that's put me on the Most Wanted posters ... it's the bringing them back! My folks have paid enough fines to send me through college. You see, I can't turn loose and let go once I get my sticky little fingers on any hardcover or paperback! I don't want to give them up   they're little printed hostages! My mom's usually the one who sets them free!

I know I'm strange to have such a book fetish, but I say it's better for my teeth (not to mention my hips) than being addicted to chocolate; better for my ears than being tuned to loud rock music; better for my soul than being a shoplifter! My all-time favorite TV show was *Ellen* — not that she was such a super actress, not that the lines were so clever, not that she finally came out of the closet — but that she had that quaint little bookstore: Buy the Book! And I loved the movie *You've Got Mail* and not because Tom Hanks turned me on ... well, he does make my heart flutter a little ... but not as much as Meg Ryan's bookstore! That's what I want to do — work for a large chain of bookstores ... just let myself get lost in the printed word.

I'm equally thrilled with people who write books — I love authors! I e-mail them to praise their work and ask for autographed pictures.

Stephen King, Judy Blume, Patricia Cornwell and Sue Grafton are just a few of the faces on my bulletin board. Maybe someday I'll write a novel … be somebody's idol … see my face on a book jacket! Well, that's it … my idiosyncrasy. I suppose you think I'm a little weird. So, what the hey … I don't need a lot of positive strokes. I don't need an army of friends. I don't need a shrink. All I need is a can of Diet Pepsi and a new Grisham novel!

Breaking Up with Tyler

Today's the day … I've got to do it … It's cruel to drag it out any longer. Yes, today's the day I break up with Tyler! It won't be easy; I've been going with him since we were in Huggies Pull-ups! Our mothers went to the same college — were sorority sisters. We're practically joined at the hip, but I need to break loose — disjoint myself. It's going to break everyone's hearts; Mom won't speak to me for months. Karen, Tyler's mother, will never look at me again — they already had their grandchildren named! Dad will be OK with it; he's said for years that Mom and Karen have been shoving us down each other's throats. It's not that I don't love Ty — I do — like a brother.

I didn't realize that till Colt walked into our geometry class. My knees turned to Jell-O, my heart raced, and my tongue was so tied in knots I couldn't tell him my name. In a flash it occurred to me that this is how I should feel when I see Tyler; instead, it's more like slipping into my old, comfortable Nikes!

The sad part is I think Ty's really in love with me. His every thought for the future involves me. He's planned our college and careers. That's why I feel like such a creep. It may leave permanent scars; he may be afraid to ever have a meaningful relationship again. It'll be like stabbing a dagger in his heart. And since I'm his one and only true love, the wound may never heal. But he needs to try — spread his wings, even if no other girl measures up to me in his eyes and heart.

So, you see why I hesitate. I know it's not fair to him or me to keep on seeing him and drooling over Colt at night. Of course, to be truthful, Colt hasn't actually shown any real interest in me, but once he knows I'm free, he'll want to check out more than my geometry answers!

"What, Mom? Who's on the phone? Sure I can talk to Tyler." Even I won't be heartless enough to break the bad news on the phone — though it is tempting, wouldn't have to see those sad puppy-dog eyes! *(Picks up phone.)* "Hi, Ty, what's up? Sure I remember that we have a

73

date tomorrow night — wouldn't miss it. I have something important to discuss with you. Yes, really important." *(Covers phone.)* Poor Sap, probably doesn't have a clue he's getting the major kiss-off! "Oh, you can't make it? Well, Ty, I really needed to see you. What's come up? Coach call an extra practice? Well, what then … your grandma have another gall bladder attack? You're being a little secretive, Tyler McPherson, that's not like you at all. You can tell me anything … What do you mean, I'm not strong?" *(Covers phone.)* This kid's going to drive me over the edge; is it any wonder I want to send him to the dumpster? "Go ahead … just say it! You're what? I don't believe it! That's not funny, Tyler. You're serious? You mean you're really … say it again, I think I misunderstood you. Well, of all the nerve, after all we've been through, after all we've meant to each other, after all I've put up with … you're dumping me?! How could you? Is there no such word as loyalty in your limited vocabulary? I gave you the best years of my life! You've completely broken my heart … This is good-bye … forever … I don't want to hear your stupid voice again!" *(Slams down phone.)* I can't believe it … you think you know someone … *(Sniffs.)* I'll never be the same … a dejected woman … Tyler — the worm — has dumped me!

Building the Perfect Male

Why can't guys be human? Why do they have to be such slobs? Why do they think of nothing but cars, sports and girls' boobs? They stand us up, flirt with all our friends (and enemies), never have enough money to treat us right, have manners from the stone age and never give us a decent compliment after hours of primping for a date. It's just too bad we can't go into a laboratory and, with only superior parts, build the perfect male. Imagine how Mary Shelley felt when she created Frankenstein! We, of course, would want our specimen to be a little more attractive. We will want to take him out in public and introduce him to our friends and make them parrot-green with envy. We will want to be able to sit across the table from him in classy restaurants and not gag on our entrée. For you see, our perfect gentleman will take us to four-star establishments — not the fast food joints where mortal guys take their dates.

Yes, I can see it now, after much research, the blueprint emerges for the ideal male. We will have programmed in perfect amounts of the necessary ingredients. good manners, muscle tone, loyalty, humor, generosity and, of course, a personality that lights up airport runways. Stir in heaping amounts of Leonardo DiCaprio's sex appeal; throw in Tom Cruise's eyes, Mel Gibson's grin, and Brad Pitt's hair, and I think we've got something! And Thomas Edison thought his lightbulb was a hot number!

We will package our product in expensive Brooks Brothers attire — no tank tops, scruffy cut-offs or smelly sweats for our straight-from-the-factory hero. We will, of course, patent our fabulous invention and stamp it with the Good-Guy-Watching Seal of Approval. This new creation will be on every girl's Christmas list — Santa better get his chubby cheeks a'crackin'!

Your ordinary, mortal guys better just hang it up ... you're born losers ... you won't stand a chance against the new, improved model!

Calling All Guys

Some girls collect teddy bears; others buy hundreds of earrings or bottle-after-bottle of weird nail polish. My best friend, Carrie, has two hundred pairs of shoes! Jessica and Jentry have stacks of CDs — I think they're all silly hobbies! I, on the other hand, collect guys! Yes, by the age of eighteen, I intend to be in the *Guiness Book of World Records* for having dated the most boys. I know it's not everyone's cup of cappuccino, but don't knock it till you've had the stamina to try it! And I don't go into such an endeavor lightly ... it's not easy to keep my dating calendar up-to-date and notarized! Though I'm out to set a record, I won't date a guy just because he marks M on the gender line of his enrollment card. I do have my standards! I want this male militia I date to be fun, clean, good dancers, taller than 5'6", non-perverts, and intelligent enough to fill out the form I've prepared for my record race!

I'm not doing this to be Miss Popularity — I could accomplish that by saying yes instead of no in the tight clinches — It's just something I decided to do. My mother suggested other records (that her bridge club ladies and the PTA could swallow easier) like wearing my hair in the most ponytails; making the most Santas from toilet paper spools; knitting the world's longest sock! But these nerdy suggestions somehow didn't turn me on like the dating game!

So, it started ... and Mom, I must say, wasn't a poor loser — she helped me with the documentation (she's a bookkeeper) and bought me mucho vitamin B-50s! She also checked out each boy's family, driver's license, and blood type! (I couldn't prove it, but I think the FBI has all of their fingerprints on file!) It became a family project — instead of watching Wheel of Fortune or doing puzzles together, we all tabulated, updated and projected my dating chart! My older brother got with the program and brought in many likely candidates; my sister wrote this ad for the school paper: "Call me a glory seeker. Call me a name dropper. Call me a trendsetter ... but call me! at (883) 555-2323 to set a dating record for the Guiness!"

My friends worried that I'd be called desperate, cheap or pushy for advertising like that. My biggest worry was that Mr. Right would pop up amid the other rejects, (You see, I limited each guy to just one date ... therein the record.) and I'd have to put him on hold till I reached my dating goal. It hasn't happened yet ... my guardian angel must have a soft spot in the romance department! I'm about there ... only need a few more numbers ... er ... ah ... dates. (I hate to admit this, but I think of my past dating lineup only as numbers.) Come on, don't think harsh thoughts about me ... I'm almost done now, and I'll have gained entry into the Book. It's caught on, the whole town's into it — I'm getting swamped with calls. Now that it's almost over, I can admit I had a fear some guys would laugh and say obscene things about me and my record-breaking plot, but it never happened. I'm sure it's because of my lady-like demeanor that made all of those dating dynamos treat me with such respect. — with kid gloves! Or maybe it's because my father's the Chief of Police!

Drivin' Ms. ... Crazy

I know girls aren't supposed to be into cars and driving like guys are, but they shouldn't be allergic to the thought of grabbing the car keys like I am. I simply don't want to drive. I do not share this thought with my friends — they'd think I need therapy or Prozac. It's a known fact — teenagers live for the day they can get behind the wheel ... and peel! Well, not me ... I'd rather walk or ride with my more adventuresome friends. It's not that I don't want to get out where the action is — I do — I just don't want to drive to it! I'm afraid of a lot of things — big dogs, heights, lightning and driving. (Maybe I *do* need therapy!)

Even my folks began to worry about my lack of interest in this teenage reverie. My sister was ashamed of me, and my brothers thought I was hopeless. But it was my Grandad who did something about it — he paid my $250 enrollment fee and signed me up for summer Drivers Ed. I wouldn't go, I locked myself in my room, held my breath — all to no avail. My relatives stood together — the first united front *ever* in this dysfunctional family — determined to get me licensed!

So, off I went the first morning. It was much the same as my first day of kindergarten. I was pushed into the stop-sign-postered room. I was hoping to look into the eyes of a sympathetic, grandfatherly (although my own grandfather was now on my Hitler list) type driving instructor. Well, I really missed the mark on that one! I looked into the sharp, Titanic-iceberg eyes of a living, breathing witch! She had red hair to her waist and a voice that would make nails scratching on blackboards a welcome sound. I knew I'd met my Waterloo. No more Father's Day cards or ashtrays for Grandpa!

There were two of us — a dweeb guy whose hands were shaking as bad as mine. The stringy-haired witch lady rushed us to the car and pointed out the driving gadgets of the school Chrysler. This Chrysler witch told us to call her Ms. ... I found out later, quite by accident, that her last name was Dumbwalk. We could have had fun with that under normal circumstances!

And so it went — Dweeb Boy and I — under the evil eye of the Broomless One. We progressed from being bug-eyed observers to back-street Chrysler operators. It was a slow, painful process — many Tylenols were consumed by all three participants. We ran over curbs, passed stop signs, went through red lights! I don't know who finished first when the course was over, we were all wrecks — me, Dweeb Muffin, Wicked Witch of the Steering Wheel ... and the Chrysler!

But I'm putting the experience behind me ... on occasion, when duty demands it, I'll get behind the wheel of a car. I don't enjoy it nor do any of my passengers, but a girl's gotta do ... and by the way, I'm speaking to my Grandpa again!

Flip a Coin

I've really got a problem — a big one. No, I didn't get cut from cheerleading tryouts ... No, I didn't get left out of the senior play cast ... No, I didn't get a zit on my nose before senior pictures ... but it's still a biggie! You see, I have to choose between two guys! Don't laugh ... it's a serious decision, and I don't want to make the wrong choice. I really wanted to string them both along, but they're both getting pushy and demanding — *Men!*

It really could have worked — me dating both guys. You see, Derek's the world's best dancer. He's the greatest date for proms and all school dances. He also likes to act; we're playing the leads in the senior play. He's just the most considerate guy. All my friends are jealous that I have him tied up ... and Brent.

They want me to turn one of them loose because there aren't that many good ones out there! They say I'm a selfish witch ... that I've got to choose! I just smile ... and say I'm going to hang on to both of them as long as I can.

Who'd want to give up Super Jock Brent? Sure, he's not as smart as Derek, but he's got that cool Corvette and his butt's so cute in his football uniform! OK, call me superficial ... I don't care — these things count when you're seventeen! I know when I'm fifty I won't care about a guy's buns or ... well, I'll still pay attention to his car! I like to think I'm not influenced by the fact that Brent's rich — he's always buying me expensive gifts. But a girl gets used to that kind of stuff ... and remember I already admitted I'm superficial!

Well, my time's about up for playing the field. Derek and Brent both want an answer — they're both too selfish to share me! I can see how they'd both want me body and soul — I was voted the cutest, sexiest senior in the yearbook's Who's Who! And, like I said, my friends are all pushing ... and licking their chops, waiting to zero-in on my leftovers! I can't stand the idea of Shelly going with my Derek ... and the thought of seeing Courtney in Brent's 'Vette makes my blood boil! See? I can't let go ... call me fickle, but my heart has a place for both of these guys ... *and* the Corvette! What if I choose one, then the next day realize I'm madly in love with the other? It'll be too late, and it might affect the rest of my senior year ... or my summer vacation!

So you see, I wasn't kidding when I said I had a *real* problem. Aren't you sorry you doubted me ... made fun? And the sad thing is ... nobody can help me. It's a decision I have to make alone. Oh, some have given advice. "Weigh the pros and cons carefully," said our wishy-washy school counselor. "Go with the money," were greedy Granny's words to the wise. *"Just pick one!"* chimed all my dateless friends. So you see, I'm on my own ... I'll sleep on it ... think about it tomorrow ... and if I still can't decide ... I'll flip a coin!

Get Well, Mrs. Walton

I guess everyone has that special teacher who made a difference ... that someone who cared enough to make you want to go to school each morning. Well, for me that teacher was Mrs. Walton, our freshmen family living (In the good old days we called it home ec.) teacher. We really learned things in this class that we could actually use — cooking, sewing, family skills, good manners, etiquette, etc. And Mrs. Walton made the class fun. She had her room so tastefully decorated, and she taught these survival skills in such a creative way — slide shows, videos, demonstrations, role playing ... and while we were preparing these presentations, we were learning to work cooperatively. We were all so anxious to get to this elective class; nobody skipped family living.

Then one day when we got there we had a substitute; we weren't too concerned — every teacher needs the occasional mental health day! And we could keep the ship afloat while Mrs. Walton got over her sniffles or whatever. But, the second day, the third day ... then the second week, and no Mrs. Walton. The sub was a weak imitation; of course, it wasn't her fault — great teachers are born, not created in college education classes. We begged for daily updates on Mrs. Walton's condition, but they never tell the sub anything. We knew it had to be serious; Mrs. Walton would never desert us without just cause. Somebody in her family must be ill ... she won a trip to Hawaii ... or better yet — the lottery! Ah, oh, Mr. Chilton, the principal ... we're in for trouble now. our conduct hasn't been so good since Mrs. Walton's been away. Oh, no, he's making an announcement ... Mrs. Walton's sick ... surgery ... chemo ... I can't believe it! She was here not so long ago, making plans for our house projects. We were going on a field trip to the Carpet Shop. She promised to be my guest at the church's Mother/Daughter Banquet. I haven't attended since Mom left. But maybe it's not so bad ... people bounce back ... and Mrs. Walton's a bouncer! There are survivors in the news every day. I'll put her on the prayer list at church, take up a collection for hospital flowers, and I'll write her a poem:

If all teachers were like you, my friend,
No kid would want the school day to end.
You taught me to think ... to cook ... to spell,
Now, one more favor — please ... please ... *get well!*

Girls Are the Superior Sex

We're getting ready for a debate in English class on the superior sex. I personally think it's no contest! Even the guys know we females are today's leaders — the real brain power. Who makes all the A's? Who makes up seventy percent of the honor roll? Who gives birth to, raises and trains all the children? We know the history books give all the credit to the males, but look who wrote those books. Now, in the modern world we find as many female writers as male — ever hear of Danielle Steel? Years ago, the ladies were too busy being pioneer women to grab a quill.

Of course, they're going to throw at us the old Adam-being-tricked-by-Eve story. Well, I say a smart man (probably an oxymoron) wouldn't have let anyone poke that Jonathan down his Adam's apple! All Eve had to do was give a little wink, a little fig-leafed shake ... and he was putty in her conniving little palm ... thereby giving females forever the upper hand!

The guys are going to say we're too flighty, too illogical! But at least we don't spend our lives watching sports on TV and working on fast cars. Females are into more intellectual pursuits like shopping, gossiping and having our nails done!

Women are just more diplomatic; we know how to get things done. We don't blunder our way through life. Sure, if the situation calls for a little kissing-up, we're the first to purse our lips! Why do you think so many teacher's pets are female? If a little backstabbing is required, a female will be there sharpening her dagger. If the blade doesn't work, we use our razor-sharp tongues to shred you guys' ideas, your arguments and your egos!

But our best weapon by far is our God-given look of innocence — there's not a female walking this planet who can't at any given moment impersonate an angel with a newly-shined halo! So, you see, you guys just don't stand a chance. Sure, you're smart sometimes, you get better-paying jobs, you're clever sometimes and on an off-day — cute ... but you don't have the cunning kind of mind that could make you superior. Your mommy knew when she was teaching you guys to be macho, independent, resourceful that it wouldn't really be enough ... 'cause no matter what, your gender will *always* come in second!

Granny's Dating

I thought as a teen I'd suffered every humiliation — gone through every crisis, but I was wrong! The Dump Fairy has handed me a new one — he's turned my grandmother into a dating dynamo! Talk about shameful ... I have to share my mirror, my eyeliner and my CK perfume with a sixty-plus teenager! I've heard of second childhood, but who'd ever suspect my once level-headed, cookie-baking grandma would be going through that stage. I was sympathetic with her hot flashes, trotted out to get her estrogen refills, but I'm not very understanding when she's fluttering around, borrowing my earrings so she'll look sexy for her date!

I can't figure out how it happened — Granny went from grief counseling to the Dating Game in one swift stroke! One minute she was folding Grandpa's clothes for the Salvation Army, the next she was folding Victoria's Secret undies! Mom says she's going through a phase; Dad just watches his mother primping and sets curfews which Gram ignores. I personally think she's flipped ... lost it ... Bonkersville! She used to spend her evenings playing bridge and going to church socials — now she's out on the town four or five times a week. She used to sing gospel music in the shower — now she belts out "I'm a merry, merry widow ..." then laughs!

I will admit one thing, she's lots more fun to shop with, now that she's "out among 'em" (her phrase for her new lifestyle). We spent three hours yesterday finding nail polish — all the new glitzy stuff really turns Granny on! Her toenails sparkle like sequins, and with her new open-toed sandals, they draw lots of attention. (Granny used to wear old lady shoes — she was a librarian, for heaven's sake!) Now we go to all the style shows ... and I'll admit since she became a Glamour Gram my wardrobe has really perked up. She'll say, "Let's buy you this tight blouse ... I might want to borrow it!" I think her conscience is biting her a bit spending Grandpa's pension checks on dating duds! But we shop and laugh and throw Grandpa's money around like it was confetti on New

86

Year's Eve!

I'm really not too fond of Gram's new beaus. Personally, I think she could do better — if she insists on dating, but I still cast a vote for her sitting at home in a rocking chair drinking Ovaltine ... like all the other grandmothers! One old geezer is so frail I'm afraid he'll expire while he's driving his '82 Chevy to bingo. Another is so cheap! He makes Grandma pay her own way. I know what he's after ... the pension checks! The latest is fifteen years younger ... now that's a real disgrace! I actually ran into them at the movies — they were holding hands! I'm supposed to be the one everybody's worried about. It's not fair — she's had her day, it's my time now! I should have center stage ... not my over-the-hill-but-still-kicking Grandma!

Granny's Gone

My grandmother died today, and she was very special to me. She was more than a cookie baker, a dress maker, a problem solver — she was the best friend I ever had. My friends couldn't believe that I could talk about anything with Granny. This old gal was a great listener, and she gave excellent advice. She didn't faint and quote the Bible like my other grandma. She didn't always agree with me, and she told me when I was wrong, but she did it in such a way that I learned something and didn't get mad. She had such a sense of humor, too. We'd laugh over crazy things till we cried — she was one-in-a-million, and now she's gone. And to make matters worse, today's her birthday; she would have been sixty-seven — not so old by today's standards, but leukemia doesn't consider age.

This is a box of stuff she left for me — had my name on it, and taped real tight. I think it's mostly old jewelry and poetry books. Granny and I shared a love for good poetry ... oh, look ... her old report cards! A's in subject matter, C's in conduct! You kept secrets from me, Granny. Oh, look, it's a diary ... so old, and the lock is broken. Let's see, yep, it's your handwriting, Granny ... and it's when Dad was a kid ... um, sounds like he was a pill! Misconduct must run in the family. Dad, if you get on my case if I get called to the principal's office, I can say it's just in my genes!

This was all written when Gramps was in the army ... guess you had a lot of free time on your hands, Granny ... looks like you and Dad were having fun: two of you at the beach, Gram and Dad, Gram and Dad, Gram and Dad and *Fred Dillon!* What's this? Oh, Gram, you really should have burned this! Gram and Fred ... I remember him — tall, head as bald and shiny as a bowling ball ... always helping Gramps ... oh, boy ... Granny, how could you? Maybe ... nobody's perfect? Really, Granny, the report cards would have been enough! I wonder what happened? Oh, boy ... well, I guess Scarlett had her Ashley ... Katherine Hepburn had Spencer Tracy ... and maybe Granny had ... Fred!

What, Dad? No, I'm OK. I'll be coming right down ... no, there wasn't anything of interest in the box ... You owe me one, Granny!

Guys Give Me Hives

I think mothers of teenage boys are really missing the pontoon. Instead of sending caring, gentlemanly young men into the world, they're shipping out selfish, boastful, show-offish cads! Now, I'm not saying every creature out there with Bic nicks on his chin is a total wash-out, but let's face it, guys, you need work! (And I've found that to most of you, work is a four-letter word!)

The male gender falls into categories — Super Jocks, Geeks, Trouble Makers, and just plain old Dweebs. I'll admit sometimes there is a little overlap, but for the most part you guys are pretty much labeled.

Now you Dweebs know who you are and so does every female on the planet. You aren't so bad to look at — you just need to spruce up and grow up! Give up the computer games and practical jokes — being a clown only worked in middle school, so pack up the old rubber chicken and whoopie cushion 'cause you're in the real world now!

Calling all Trouble Makers ... I'm not saying we're not a little attracted to guys who live on the edge, but we girls want to know our steady dates aren't spending big blocks of time in the principal's office, in or out of school detention, or in jail! We like your ruggedness, your spirit of adventure, your daring ... but we'd like you better if you gave up the tough-guy image and cleaned up your vocabulary!

Now that we're living in a world of technology, you Geek Guys are coming into your own. I've no doubt when we have our ten-year reunion, you'll all be hailed as the most successful, wealthiest alumni. But to enhance your remaining days in high school, here are a few helpful hints — cut the goofy laugh, burn the suspenders, invest in contact lenses and bury the old horn-rimmed glasses.

And last but in their minds not least — the Super Jocks who think you rule the earth ... a little too good for regular air, water or girls. We know someday you'll outgrow this look-at-me-I'm-so-cool attitude, but we'll have to wait till you're through college and the applause of past glories on the field has dwindled to echoes in your mind. Now, I ask you, who has that kind of time — most of us earth girls want a boyfriend now!

So there you have it — I hope you learned something, fellas. It's not too late ... you can shake off your labels. Yep, with just a little effort you can slither out of your old skin and become real human beings!

Hear Them Bells

Yes, wedding bells ... and if you're going to lecture me — say I'm too young, haven't lived yet — you're too late, I've heard it all! But I'm still going to do it. In a few minutes I'll be marching down the aisle on Dad's arm — it won't be the first time he's given me away. When he walked out on my mom for another woman, for all practical purposes, he gave me away then. Gone were our camping trips, bike rides, one-on-one basketball matches. Mostly though, *gone* was my dad — my pal, my best friend, the love of my life. So, I'll really just be borrowing the arm today for a few minutes then it goes back to his new wife, Marcie, forever.

The whole world's against my upcoming marriage — not that they don't like Tony, but everyone thinks we should go to college first. No, I don't *have* to get married like Pam and Lora ... I just want to! I love Tony ... we belong together, and he's going to school, working evenings at Wal-Mart. I have a good job at the bank, and we have the cutest little apartment. It'll be like playing house — cooking, doing laundry, cleaning our place! Mom says this desire to play Betty Crocker will wear off in two weeks ... maybe sooner! But I know we'll be so happy; I don't care what anybody says. I'm not *at all* jealous of my friends with their new college wardrobes, their pledge dreams, their career expectations! I have what I want! I am a little jittery ... just bridal nerves.

Oh, no, there go the bridesmaids; it's almost my turn. I know I'm not making a mistake ... this is what I really want. Mom said she'd stop the music at any time ... I just need to say the word. She has plenty of stamps to return the gifts. But I can't change my mind now — I've got the old ... new ... borrowed ... blue paraphernalia strung up and down my body! The flowers are paid for. The cake with the midgets on top is sitting on the table. The bald minister is holding the Bible.

You know, college would have been kind of fun ... parties, sororities, dorm life. Come out of it, girl, you gave up all that when you squeezed that tiny, tiny diamond on your finger. Remember, making a greasy meatloaf, folding underwear, and cleaning the dirty toilet has a certain charm, too! Could I possibly have been wrong this time ... and *everybody else* right? Did I have such a strong case of senioritis I became stone deaf to all the good advice from people whose opinion I normally respected?

Ohhh ... the music ... they're playing my song. Here's Dad and that traitorous arm. I can see Tony down there looking nervous ... and *young* ... so young ... too young! What have I done to him? To myself? It was mostly my fault. He wanted to wait. Well, here goes. I'm off ... left foot first ... I think it will be OK ... I hope ... just a bad case of stage fright. You know, for once I wish I'd listened to Mom. Too late now 'cause here comes the bride!

Jenny's Not Eating ... Again

Jenny's mother looks terrible again; I can tell she's back on her nerve pills, and I'll bet she's not sleeping ... and who can blame her when her daughter, my best friend, Jenny, has an eating disorder?

Jenny wants to eat better ... She hates making herself and her family sick, but she just can't help it. We have long talks about her eating habits ... It's been going on for three years now. Her folks have had her in counseling, flown her to eating disorder specialists, but still Jenny has food problems. Whenever she passes a mirror, Jenny always says, "Look how fat I am!" This is coming from a string bean! I point out the flatness of her stomach, how her hips are nothing but bones while mine are as round as Moon Pies. I've read up on anorexia, and know what a disabling disease it is. But I don't know how my best friend ever got it!

Three years ago we were happy-go-lucky junior high students looking forward to taking on high school with gusto! We were practicing for drill team tryouts, spent hours updating our wardrobes, and were anxious to start guy watching! But it didn't work out that way. Jenny lost so much weight she was sick most of her freshman year; she went from a size eight to a two! It happened so fast, I didn't see it coming. One day we were eating Peanut Buster Parfaits at Dairy Queen, and the next she wasn't eating anything! She'd always say she'd had a snack at home, or she had cramps, or her mom was fixing a big dinner. She was upset during this time because her mom and dad split up, and Jenny was a real Daddy's girl. But I never thought she'd develop an eating disorder.

By our sophomore year, Jenny had collapsed twice at school and was taken to Charter for treatment. I visited her in the hospital and was happy to see her eating. Her mom said she was doing better. When she came back to school, Jenny was quiet; she seemed to have lost her zest for school, friends and life in general. She was still seeing her therapist and I was glad. We still talked on the phone, but it was mostly a one-sided conversation.

Things started looking up in our junior year — Jenny fell in love. Brian was the best thing that ever happened to Jenny. She started going to school functions, smiling, and her weight seemed to improve. She was more like the old fun-filled girl I'd always known. I could see relief in her mom's eyes. But in the middle of our senior year, Brian dumped her for Shelly, the new girl in school. Within weeks Jenny became a shadow. Her mom called me ... Jenny refused to see her therapist, wasn't eating and had lost all interest in her classes. Two weeks before graduation, Jenny took an overdose of sleeping pills. Luckily, her mom found her in time ... She's in the hospital now. There was an empty space in the lineup when they played "Pomp and Circumstance." Jenny and I had such high hopes for college together. Now, I'm not sure when she'll be released, or if she can make it on her own. Eating disorders are not a passing fad ... not an extended diet ... they're a serious problem. If you know somebody with this affliction, *please* get her help. I pray every night that my friend Jenny will overcome this disorder and get on with her life.

Laughing on the Outside

My favorite pastime is looking through catalogs — at skinny girls — and wishing I could look like them instead of buying my clothes at the Short and Chunky Shop. Oh sure, I make fun of myself — crack jokes about how many fields it took to yield up enough cotton balls to weave me a pair of extra large jeans! I'm the first one to say I bring my lunch in a Hefty bag. I get lots of laughs ... mine is the first and the loudest. You see, I've learned one thing — when you make fun of yourself, it cushions the blow, and it doesn't hurt so much when others laugh at you. Oh, it still hurts, don't get me wrong, nobody likes to be the butt of the joke, but you learn to grin and bear it.

I wasn't always chubby. My baby pictures show a happy, thin little girl. I like to look at those skinny legs and wonder how many french fries, Dunkin' Donuts, pound bags of M&Ms it took to plump them up like stuffed sausages. It's not all my fault. My grandma's fat, my mom's more than on the heavy side, so I just cop out, grab a Mars bar and say, "It runs in the family." But my older sister has a Julia Roberts' figure; she has the same genes, sat at the same carbohydrated table and came out looking like a model! Sandy does pass up the potatoes every time and goes heavy on the salad. She never has desserts and works out every evening at the gym. She's tried to help me, but she does it with such a snooty attitude I just grab another roll, douse it with butter and plunk it in my mouth. Mom says it's just a phase, and I'll outgrow it — the growing part is what scares me. I've already grown from a size twelve to a sixteen in a year!

It's not that I'm not popular ... sort of. I'm really a hanger-on ... somebody who's always there to boost the morale of the in crowd. Of course, I never try out for cheerleader, or drill team, or the Jazz Dance Corp. The sad thing is, I'd be good at all of them — I have great rhythm, energy and enthusiasm. I got brave my freshman year and gave drill team a shot. I had the numbers down, a fresh haircut, new shorts, etc., but I could just see the judges looking at my dimpled knees, my fuller chest, and I knew it was hopeless. There's such prejudice out there, even with the adults, and it's not just the color of one's skin; it's how much skin it takes to cover the body! Roseanne and Oprah made it being fat, but they didn't stay that way — they spent big bucks to get their bodies reduced and reshaped! Needless to say, I went home from the tryouts in total defeat.

It's not that I haven't tried all the fad diets — the roof of my mouth is still sore from drowning myself in grapefruit juice. And next week I've got an appointment with a doctor, and I've signed up to go to the gym. Maybe there's a slim future out there for me ... if not, until people get over their prejudice against heavy people, I'll just have to come up with some more fat jokes to tell on myself!

Lookin' for Mr. Right

I know the tender age of eighteen is too young to start husband hunting. I would never want to be saddled with housework, a husband and screaming kids before I had a life — tried my wings. But it's never too soon to start to look and observe — listen and learn. Because I'm sure someday (after I've become a whiz bang lawyer and put all the bad guys in jail) I'll want to settle down, snatch up one of the few remaining good guys and raise a lovely family. So, I'm preparing a notebook: wants/not-wants, pros/cons, dos/don'ts in selecting the ideal husband.

I've read some of the many books on the subject; I've watched my Oprah — so, I've got a good idea of what I don't want in my future mate. I don't want him to be controlling — I've seen this ugly trait in my own father. He wants everything his way. We buy what he wants, eat what he likes, go where he drives. No, thanks. Mom may have to put up with it, but not me! I also don't want a guy with a bad temper — Uncle John blows up over everything, scaring his kids and giving Aunt Ellen an ulcer. I don't want somebody who's stingy — my grandfather squeezes every penny, making Granny wear garage sale clothes and shop at dollar stores. So, I've observed several qualities I want to avoid in my own special guy. But there are some musts on my shopping list, too. For instance, I want him to be sweet, caring, and have a good sense of humor. I'd like it if he'd be one of the few guys who can put someone else's feelings before his own. It wouldn't hurt if he was nice-looking, well-educated, and had a little muscle tone. I'm not kidding myself into thinking there are a million super heroes out there just waiting for me to take my pick!

Then, too, I'm afraid I won't recognize Mr. Right when he passes my way! I've seen all the old romance movies — bells ringing, music playing, eyes meeting across a crowded room! I'd really like for my true love to sweep in and carry me away ... like Richard Gere in *An Officer and a Gentleman*! But what if, when our special moment arrives, my soul mate's turned the other way ... tying his shoe and I just walk on by ... out of his life? It's something to worry about.

Of course, I've had lots of tips and helpful hints in my quest for the ideal man. My friend Sonja and my grandmother cast their votes for money — Gram says "Even if you're miserable, you can suffer in comfort!" My Family Living teacher says mutual interests and compatibility are what really counts. The minister says find a man of the faith. Aunt Sophia says "Check his teeth." My folks want me to land one who's dependable. And my friends all say to wait till I find a guy who makes my legs turn to Silly Putty!

I'm sure all of this advice is good ... and I'll sure consider all the facts and fantasies. Like I've said before, I'm not in any rush. I just want to research all the possibilities ... and be ready ... so I'll be able to recognize and latch onto Mr. Right when he comes my way!

Miss America or Bust

You heard me, one day I'll be Miss America — it's written in the stars, in the family album, in my baby book! My mom is the ultra backstage mother. She was making tutus for me when I was in the womb. I've been in every baby contest since leaving the hospital. In fact, Mom tried to get me out-on-leave on my second day for the Silver Spoon Baby Contest, but my pediatrician put his foot down. Needless to say, we have a new doctor and my mom holds the old one personally responsible for my having an empty space in my Awards Scrapbook!

My childhood wasn't like other girls'. I wasn't allowed out in the sun — no swimming or afternoon parties in the park where I might get exposed to the sun or germs! I couldn't have gone anyway because I spent my afternoons and weekends at dance lessons, piano lessons, twirling lessons and voice lessons. It's a good thing my father's a lawyer! There's a whole closet in my basement for my outfits. (Mom keeps them because she says, "Someday you'll have a little girl ..." and the cycle can go on and on and on ...) At the drop of a hat I can be Auntie Em's little Dorothy (I even have a stuffed Toto ... no time for real pets in my busy life.), a Spice Girl, or turn my dimples on and sail away on the *Good Ship Lollipop*! I'm always prepared — though Brownies and Girl Scouts were another no-no.

It wouldn't be so bad if I had a sister — or even a brother, but there was no time to think about a sibling for me ... it might have interfered with my performance schedule. Now, Dad has tried to slow Mom down, but he didn't stand a chance ... I was destined to be all that I can be and nothing or nobody has been allowed to stand in my way. Luckily, I'm a good student, and with the tutor Mom hired and her relentless campaign to get me "gifted" status, I've been able to test out of many classes. I'll graduate next year when I'm barely seventeen.

I'm not saying I hate my life ... I just need to *get* one! When I'm a little down, Mom just reminds me that I'm spoiled — had too many advantages, and I hear the old "If I'd had only half your chances" story. Sometimes I wonder what it would be like to have a normal, girl-next-door life — slumber parties, chatting and giggling with girlfriends on the phone for hours, shopping at girl shops for things in denim (instead of sequined costume shops), or just hangin' out with a group of friends. Well, it's too late for any of that ... the die is cast and I'm headin' for the big time — and along the way I'm Miss America bound.

Mom's Expecting

Who'd ever have guessed that I'd be waiting outside the delivery room — for, of all people, my *mother* to have a baby! When they told me she was pregnant, I laughed and said, "Good one, Mom!" Sure, when I was four I wanted a sister, but not when I'm seventeen! Talk about being humiliated! I refused to go to public places with my mother after she started wearing maternity clothes. I begged her to stay away from teacher conferences and other school functions. I quit bringing my friends home — my whole life's changed, and the baby's not even here yet!

It's just not fair ... I'm the one doing the suffering. Mom's as happy as a cop with a new book of traffic tickets. And Dad's swaggering around like he discovered electricity ... or Viagra! I'm only going to say this once — I don't even want to *think* of my folks and the s-e-x word! I'm really the only one looking at this situation with an open mind. These parents of mine are used up ... damaged merchandise. They don't have the strength, the guts, the endurance, the patience to go through all those childhood phases again. Cripes, Mom should be preparing for menopause, not a baby shower. She needs to be investing in estrogen, not Johnson & Johnson! What's the world coming to?

I will admit physically, socially and mentally my expectant parents came through all of this pretty well — can't say the same for yours truly! Yep, for an over-the-hill preggie, Mom did OK. Oh, well, she did the breakfast barf for a few weeks, and lately the constant trudges to the little girls' room — talk about a weak bladder! She said she was showing me the dark side of pregnancy — so I'll stay a virgin!

I still don't know how they'll manage this baby on their busy schedules. It's been a struggle for Mom to get to all my games and performances. I never count on Dad — he always has to see the video. I know Mom has a six weeks' leave of absence from her law office ... and I know Dad won't be able to get away from the agency — the FBI keeps people hoppin'! So, who does that leave? Grandma Sowers isn't going to be sucked away from her swingin' condo in Florida to babysit some squalling brat. She's too busy with her over-sixty single life to visit us at Christmas. And Grandma Reed forgets to take her medicine, wears mismatched shoes and thinks her middle name is Princess! So, who's going to be there to rock this baby, to treat its diaper rash, burp it like a Tupperware bowl? Oh, no ... that only leaves ... no ... no way ... not *me!* They can't expect me to raise this kid ... I'm not a finished product yet myself! I refuse to be a live-in babysitter! Well, they can just think again ... I've got a life! And it doesn't include a Pampers pooper! If they didn't have the time to take care of it, they should have considered adoption. I doubt that I'll even like it — new babies are so red and ugly. Kari's little sister looked like a boiled lobster for nine months. I'll tell you this much, I won't get attached to it ... I'd rather have a cocker spaniel!

Oh, here comes Dad ... He's carrying something ... Oh, look ... it's the baby! It's in a pink blanket ... it's a girl! I've got a sister, can you believe it? Oh, she's sooo cute ... my friends will be so jealous. Look, her eyes are just like mine ... and her forehead — a mini-me! "Let me hold her ... Dad, be careful of her head, you've got a lot to learn about babies!" Come here, Sweetie, you don't ever have to worry ... Your big sister's going to take very good care of you!

Mom's Not
Around Anymore

We buried Mom yesterday ... and I thought I was ready to give her up, but I was wrong! She'd been sick for a long time, and really didn't want to suffer any more, but I didn't want to lose her either. I keep telling myself she's just away ... like when she went to Chicago every summer to visit Aunt Patsy. But heaven's a lot farther than Chicago and they don't sell round-trip tickets!

It's just not fair to be left without a mother — I'm only sixteen years old. Who's going to help me with my dating problems? Who'll be there to get me ready for the prom or my wedding? Who's going to ever love me that much again? I'm really trying not to be mad at God for taking her ... I know He doesn't make mistakes, but maybe this time ...

It's so quiet now. All the relatives and friends have gone back to their normal lives, but mine will never be normal again. The house is alive with plants and flowers — fragrant reminders of death. The freezer and refrigerator are stuffed with funeral foods. Dad and I won't have to cook for months — assuming we get so we can eat. Aunt Polly's in the den writing thank you notes and Dad went back to work. They say keeping busy is the answer, but personally I don't think there is an answer. I'll go back to school tomorrow ... My friends have been great. But they don't really understand — 'cause they can go to the arms of caring mothers and mine will never hug me again. I hope I never get sick — 'cause who'd bring me medicine, read to me, put her cool hand on my fevered forehead? I already had her Christmas present — a birthstone pin, amethyst ... She'll be wearing it through eternity ... I hope she likes it.

Here's Mom's desk; she spent a lot of time at her computer. She was a writer. What talent ... her readers will miss her, too. Dad says we'll go through these drawers together some evening ... when it gets easier. When will that be? Nothing'll ever be easy again.

Look at all these envelopes ... My name's on all of them ... Oh, my ... oh, my ... and there's a note on top in Mom's flowery handwriting...

"To my BEAUTIFUL daughter, Misty. I'm so sorry, Darling, I can't be around for the big moments in your life, but in a small way I'll be there with these letters. I've tried to jot down some profound bits of advice in these envelopes to help you through the rough times and help celebrate the special events. I suppose I'm a little selfish, too, wanting to keep my memory alive in your heart. You're a lovely daughter, Misty, and a very special girl. I love you and I'll be watching over you from above ... Much love, ... Mom.

Oh, Mom ... I won't need these letters to keep you alive. But I'm sooo glad to have them ... and through these messages you'll be around ... to help the first time I fall in love ... on my wedding day ... when I have your first grandchild. It won't be like having you, Mom, but it will be like having a little part of you ... and Mom, I love you, too ... and ... Mom, thanks!

Nailed ... Maybe Jailed

Oh no! Mom's on the way ... I hope she didn't call Dad. I can't believe I got caught shoplifting! Shelly was right beside me with her pockets stuffed, and she waltzed out like Mary Poppins. Joni saw them nab me, and she put her loot back on the shelf. Sonja paid for her hot items ... first time in three years! But me, I'm sitting here like a wanted poster ad ... waiting for my mother and maybe the police!

I don't know how it happened ... I'm always so careful. I've got the fastest take technique ... Houdini could have used me as an apprentice. But I got caught! Mom will kill me ... Dad will ground me till I'm thirty. I'll be banned from all the shops, my face will go up in the post office, everybody at school will know I'm a felon!

The manager was really rude to me ... guess you can't blame him; I *was* stealing his stuff. I didn't really need those fake nails and polish. I have great nails of my own — it was the challenge ... the hype to see if I could get by with it. The old "everybody does it" is true, but that'll never cut it with my folks. I've had the peer pressure lecture till my ears are full! I had no idea I'd feel so bad when I got caught ... I had no idea I'd *get* caught! I know all teens think they're invincible ... that's why we drive fast, drink too much and shoplift! Well, I guess we're not unconquerable — Ken was killed on his motorcycle ... Kalab will always be in a wheelchair for driving under the influence ... and here I sit, a common thief! Oh, no, Mom will tell Aunt Patsy; she'll be so disappointed in me ... she'll be sorry I'm named after her. All for some plastic nails! Am I stupid or what? Well, it wasn't just the crummy fingernails — I wanted to look cool to the others — be a sport (Idiot's more like it!). My older sister warned me about my sticky fingers, but I just figured she was jealous because my crowd was more popular than her bookwormy friends. She even refused to wear the earrings I'd lifted to match her new outfit. I called her a goody-goody ... but I'm having second thoughts now. Guess I'll deserve her "I told you so!" I hope she comes to see me when I'm behind bars.

Well, there's Mom; she's talking to the manager. She's *not* smiling. I could turn on the tears ... appeal to her soft side! She doesn't look like she *has* a soft side today! Well, I asked for it ... I did something that's wrong, and my whole family's ashamed. I didn't think about that ... I didn't think — period! Well, I'll take my punishment and not complain ... and I'll never, never shoplift again. She's motioning for me to join them ... come on, hands, you too ... It's really all your fault ... now you're going to be fingerprinted.

Play's the Thing

If you've ever been in a production, performed a dance, sung a song, given a monolog ... you know what I'm going through — opening night jitters! In just a few minutes that curtain's going up, and I'll have to remember and *say* all those lines! What lines? I can't remember a one ... oh, no ... my mind's blank! The prompter will have the biggest part — my part! Oh, and I've got to go to the bathroom ... and I need a barf bag! Why did I think I'd ever want to be an actress? I should have stuck to painting the sets ... sewing the costumes. Now, calm down ... look at all the other actors. Don't see them fainting. Well, Henry's got his head in the trash can ... but Henry's always doing something peculiar. You know actors are a strange lot!

I was so nervous trying out for this part — Ms. Uptight, in this awesome musical comedy, "Fifties Flashback." I just knew I didn't stand a chance — the director, Ms. Keeley, doesn't like me! But I practiced ... and practiced ... and guess what? I was brilliant! And miracle of miracles, I got this juicy part of a pushy, controlling secretary who has a mad crush on her boss ... and who also gets to talk to Elvis! Now, standing here with my knees knocking, my bladder ready to explode, my stomach full of sparrows. (Butterflies just don't cut it!) I wonder why I went to all that trouble. I'm going to embarrass myself, mess up cues for the rest of the cast, ruin Ms. Keeley's play, shame my parents, and get a bad critique in the local paper!

OK, I've got to calm down ... the play only lasts ninety minutes. I only have forty-two lines — *only* forty-two? I don't know any ... except when I hear Elvis talking to me and I say, "I'm a big fan now, Elvis." But what about the other forty-one lines? And the song — my solo! I forgot about the song ... the cute little song, "I Want Romance," that I sing because I want to do a little kissy-face with the principal, Mr. Wannabeboss! Oh, dear, it *was* a cute little song during rehearsal ... now, I know I'll mess it up ... and Mr. Scarrow, the dopey chorus teacher, worked so hard with me. The group finale, "Fifties Magic," won't be so bad — the others can cover for me. You don't suppose they're as nervous as I am? I'll just slip out the back door ... who'd notice? Oh heck, Ms. Keeley's standing guard there.

Well, I look OK for my first scene — I'm a tough-talkin', take-charge gal ... and here's my poodle skirt. Whew, I think it's all coming back. I remember all my lines ... and my song! The curtain's going up, the spots are on, I know my first line! I can't wait to get out there and grab a little limelight — break a leg — 'cause the show must go on! Here I come, ready or not ... my debut ... enter Stage Left. Wow, I'm going on ... I'm really doing it — I'm an actress! Watch out, world, here comes Ms. Uptight and she's gonna be great!

Prom Queen

I'm sooo nervous ... tonight's the night. I either get the crown or I don't! Brad says I'm a shoo-in, but what does he know; he's my steady guy — what else is he going to say? I've done all the right things — bought the perfect gown, kissed up to all the right people. This compulsion to be Prom Queen wasn't just a sudden whim on my part, I actually started the crown campaign when I was six and got my first tiara. I didn't want to be in beauty pageants, have my face on magazines, be a movie star ... no, I just wanted to be Prom Queen!

My first step toward my goal was drilling all babysitters on exactly how Prom Queens are chosen. You see, each school has its own unique method of selection. Some let the faculty choose the prom royalty ... A few sports-minded schools actually let the football team elect the reigning queen ... Often, it's an out-and-out election. Well, our school has its own system — to be eligible one has to have a 3.5 GPA. Then, all organizations nominate candidates. From this list the student body narrows the possibilities to three would-be queens ... leaving the faculty the honor of choosing the Prom Queen and her two attendants. So, with such a lengthy process, you see why it's taken me my whole twelve years in the school system to be one of these top three! I've had to suck-up to teachers, administrators, not to mention every kid who could hold a voting pencil! It's not been easy, being Miss Congeniality throughout my school career. I couldn't afford to have a *best* friend — all voters were my friends. I couldn't be selective at birthday parties — all potential ballot-stuffers were invited! Sometimes I wanted to just chuck it all and be myself — throw a few tantrums, tell off some people, skip an occasional class. But then, I'd look up at the shelf and see the *tiara* and know all the smiling, all the compliments, all the bribes were worthwhile.

The teachers were pushovers. They're so used to being treated like scum by the students they're putty in the hands of a pro like me. A few kind words about their mismatched attire, sitting in the front row with

110

homework completely and correctly done, a few gifts — fruit baskets, homemade fudge, bookmarks (A ten dollar bill makes a great one!) or a personalized poem, and of course, gazing worshipfully up to them with a "You're-a-Greek-god-ready-to-reveal-ancient-secrets-to-me" look works every time.

I did have to draw the line when it came to dating. I could not, would not go out with every weirdo creep who called — even for the sake of the almighty vote. I did try to make it up to these strange-os by being their lab partner, sitting by them in homeroom, and giving them my best Meg Ryan smile!

Now is the moment of truth ... did all the sacrifices pay off? Here come the judges ... they're coming my way ... calm down, girl ... they had to come this way — it's where the microphone is ... where the stage is ... where the three candidates are! Oh, look ... one has the *tiara* ... and it's just my size! I hope I can hold down my lunch. If I don't win I hope I don't make a complete ass of myself — grab the *tiara* and run for the nearest airport! Ms. Woodworth's smiling at me ... perhaps it's just that nervous tic acting up again ... or wait, it could be a sympathy smile! No, not after the Elmo Beanie Baby I gave her (Her only grandchild is a dog — Elmo.) and Mr. Conners just winked at me! That's a good omen ... or else he has something in his eye. Take a deep breath, girl, it'll all be over in a few seconds, and you can get on with your life. Just think, either way — win or lose — you can be a normal kid for once. No more trying to impress people; you can just be yourself, so you can't lose. Mrs. Abbey is walking over with the *tiara* ... oh, no, she's stopping at Haley ... I like Haley and she deserves the title ... but ... oh, good, she's moving away ... no, no, it's Traci who'll be crowned ... and she's a lovely girl, nobody is sweeter than Traci ... oh, no ... oh ... my ... gosh ... I can't believe it — the *tiara* ... it's being placed on my head ... a perfect fit! All my efforts haven't been in vain ... Oh, yes, the mike ... "I do want to thank you all so much, I don't deserve this great honor ... never, never in a million years did I ever *dream* I'd one day be Prom Queen!"

Room for Rent

I'm not really sure I can do it — leave this room behind. It's been my sanctuary for ten years. I was so excited when Dad let me have first choice of rooms in our new house, and I got to decorate it the way I wanted. Mom made those curtains with the bright sunglasses print. I'd like to take this whole room with me; I'm going to miss this corner that I've made into a phone booth. Dad built the walls and seat — my seat's spent many hours plunked on this stool, spreading the word, passing the gossip. At least I get to take my phone — couldn't live without my phone, and Dad gave me a phone card *and* a Visa of my very own! What a guy; of course, he did set limits — nobody's perfect — even Daddykins!

Take a look at this west wall; it's become one giant bulletin board — covered with ticket stubs, old corsages, certificates and most of all, pictures — a Kodak story of my life. I'll probably take a few with me, but my dorm room has hardly any wall space, and Stacy will hog most of that with her precious celebrity pictures. This first bunch is all in the family — the five of us on all the Chevy Chaseless vacations! I'll never admit it, but I'll probably miss the twins — ornery little rugrats that they are! I've already asked Dad to put a padlock on this door so they won't move in and destroy it.

Oh, I'd forgotten I had a picture of Grandpa when he was in the hospital — such a clown, wearing all those wild wigs after losing his hair. I sure miss his phone calls and his great laugh.

Wow, look at all the weird pictures of the Mighty Five! We've been best friends since kindergarten. Now, we're breakin' up ... at least Stacy's going to the University with me. Chris's off to New York to become an actress. Dina's going to live at home for a year and help out since her Mom left. She'll go to the local junior college. And Jenna, the brightest of the bunch, is off to pre-med at Yale. But we'll all get together on holidays — and till our fathers start yelling about phone bills, let our fingers do a lot of walking.

112

Look at all the holes here — it's the space I use for the boyfriend *du jour.* I didn't realize I'd made so many punctures in the wall ... and a few in my heart! Yes sirree, there's been quite an array of male mug-shots filling this spot ... "out, damned spot!" ... it worked — look, no picture there now! But once upon a time there was Kyle — till I outgrew him (mentally and physically!) Then came Jason — Mr. Perfect — he outgrew me! He was followed by Ted, Ben, Christopher, Justin, Matt and Alex — wow, a cast of thousands! But the billboard is blank now; I'm starting college with a clean romance slate. Of course, I'm looking forward to filling my small wall space with pictures of jocks and frat boys!

So, maybe leaving this room won't be so hard after all — I'll be back for visits, but I'm just a little afraid ... afraid I'll feel like a guest ... afraid when I close this door, I'm closing the door on my girlhood. This room knows me so well ... it has shared my triumphs and defeats — my laughter and tears ... luckily there was a good balance. It was a great room to grow up in ... but I've come as far as I can here ... time to move on ... no looking back. So, farewell, old friend ... old room of my childhood!

Roommate from Hell

I was excited about going to summer camp. I know a seventeen year old should have outgrown summer camp. I'm not really a late bloomer, I'm a senior counselor! Yes, I'm one of the bigwigs, and best of all — I get paid! And *really* best of all — male counselors inhabit this camp! So, you see, there's no major character flaw with my anxiety to be at camp.

My biggest concern was my roommate — we couldn't choose our own — they were assigned from on high! I got to cabin number eleven and found my roommate had already arrived. She had the bottom bunk made up with her orange spread and all the wall space covered with doggie posters. The only dressing table was covered with pictures of *her*! "Hi, I'm Tessa, guess we're roomies," I smiled as I dropped my bags on the floor.

And she replied, without even looking up, "You know, Tessa, I specifically asked for a private room ... had I known I had to share a little cracker box like this I would have spent the summer at my family's beach house." After she said that I knew right away it was going to be a loooong summer.

After the kids arrived and camp got under way, I'd like to say the atmosphere in number eleven improved, but I can't! Heather used all the drawers but one ... and the tiny closet was stuffed with her expensive shorts sets. Luckily I only needed a corner for my cut-offs and T-shirts. Her cosmetics took up the only shelf in the cramped bathroom ... but again, I only need a spot for my lip gloss and brush. I knew I could live with Heather's grabbiness of our room — it was her attitude, her personality (or lack of one) that ticked me off.

I tried to avoid contact with my irritating roommate whenever possible. But, it was a small camp ... she whined at my lunch table; at evening council meetings she always managed to sit by the cute guy in number sixteen that I had my eye on. She never did her share of the chores; she refused to do night duty, making the rest of us have to cover.

She played her CD player so loud I had to wear ear plugs. I begged for other dwellings, but we had a No Vacancy sign over the counselors' quarters. I was sure she'd drop out — move back to her rich girl summer place, but she stayed. She whined, she complained, she griped ... but she stayed!

She insulted my haircut, my wardrobe, my outlook, my polishless nails and my complete lack of class! She dominated the TV, the shower, the air conditioner, the mirror and the alarm clock! Everything was in tune with her schedule — her selfish life. But I do think I developed strength of character — I discovered amazing amounts of willpower, and I demonstrated unsurpassed pounds of patience. 'Cause, you see, I made it for eight weeks without decking Hateful Heather — the roommate from Hell!

Shop Till Granny Drops

Today's the day I've been dreading all week — shopping with my Grandma! It's not that I don't appreciate all the time and money Grams spends on me, it's just that she's so buried in the '50s she doesn't realize that fashions have changed since she shook, rattled and rolled with Elvis! If she had her way, I'd be wearing bobby sox, starched petticoats, and a ponytail!

Don't get me wrong, I love my Grandma. Without her I'd never have a stuffed closet (Grams has a hefty bank account.) and besides, for an ancient one she's really fun. I can tell her all my troubles and she even laughs at my knock-knock jokes. The bad news about the shop-out is my mom and Grams don't hit it off so well — I think it's that mother-in-law thing. Mom's afraid her former husband's mother will point out her motherly flaws ... and she resents the time spent with me — she's *not* jealous about the money so much, since the child support checks from Dad are skimpy and irregular. So, Mom says, "It's the least your father's mother can do to make up for raising such an irresponsible son!"

Well, she'll be here any minute. I've got my catalogs to show Gram what young girls are wearing in this century. We'll shop all the expensive, matronly stores first. I'll have to give in and get a blouse and maybe underwear at these shops to please Grams and her favorite saleslady. By the time we have lunch at the Country Club, and I've shared all my deep, dark secrets with her, I'll have Gram softened up and worn down till she's ripe to do some serious denting to her wallet! Yes, we'll hit the Brass Buckle, the Gap and other stores that sell my beloved Calvin Klein's. She'll put up a little struggle over the short skirts and the low-cut tops ... but she'll be so anxious to get her new Lincoln headed back to the Mason mansion she'll agree to anything.

She'll pull up in front of my house and refuse the invitation to come in ... She's not too crazy about the woman who screwed up her little boy's life. She'll kiss my cheek, slip me twenty dollars and say, "This has been so much fun, we'll have to do it again next year!" As she takes off in a cloud of expensive smoke, I'll rush in and call my best friend to come over and see my new school wardrobe. Yes, shopping with my grandmother takes courage, but it really pays off!

Spreading My Wings

Wow! Look at all the flowers ... funeral flowers ... *my* flowers ... *my* funeral! Look at all the people ... They must have let school out ... Even kids who didn't know me are here. Oh God, it's Mom ... she looks so little ... so sad ... so old ... and it's all my fault! I didn't mean to die, Mom ... Wish she could hear me. It's OK, Mom ... I'm fine now. I'm going to be an angel! She's remembering that Dad always called me his little angel ... and now it's true. I'm to blame, Mom. Everybody warned me about abusive relationships. You and Dad never liked Michael; you said he was too jealous ... too possessive ... too controlling. I was such a silly, egotistical girl; I thought that was cute — his being green with envy if another boy even spoke to me. I thought that meant he really loved me.

My friends saw Michael for what he really was ... but I didn't ... not till the end ... when it was too late. He threatened anyone who came close to me; he was even jealous of the girls I ran around with ... time I spent with them was time I wasn't spending with him. I'd laugh at him and say, "Michael, you're great, but I need other people, too! I'm a gregarious person — I need friends!" He'd just grumble and pout! I still thought it was cute, but my folks and friends didn't. I was sure he'd change ... that he'd see that I really cared for him and start feeling secure in our relationship. But the longer we dated, the more possessive he became. His temper would flare without warning; I was almost afraid of him at times. Then came the bruises — oh, he was always sorry afterwards ... he even cried. I covered up the black and blue spots — Dad has a temper too!

Finally, it was too much. I know by now, Mom, you've read all this in my diary. I decided I had to break up with Michael. I loved him but I was getting so I didn't like him. I needed breathing space — I felt smothered. I tried to be gentle ... I told him I cared, but I couldn't live with his jealousy. It was awful, Mom ... I knew he was going to hurt me — he was out of control. He needed help all along, and I realized it when it was too late. I'm safe now, Mom, but look at you and Dad; he's hurt you more than he hurt me ... my pain's over; yours is just beginning.

If I could just comfort you, Mom ... and if I could just warn all the girls out there who are in abusive relationships. *It won't get better!* Being jealous isn't a good thing, no matter how it feeds your ego. And if a guy ever hits you, or hurts you, or forces you to do anything you don't want to do — get away! Run, and never look back. This guy doesn't love you — he loves himself. I wish I'd listened ... my family wouldn't be throwing flowers on my coffin. Well, I've got to go ... bye, Mom and Dad ... you were the best parents a girl could have. I'm going to miss you both ... try to go on with your lives ... and, remember, I love you! Well, it's over ... good-bye old life ... it's time for me to look upward ... reach for the stars ... spread my wings!

Tell-a-Girl

(Speaking into phone) Oh, hello Ashley ... I'm glad you called. Have you heard about Jennifer and Tanner breaking up? ... I know, I know, guess she finally got tired of him cheating on her. ... Yeah, guys are such slime — especially my two brothers!

... Of course I heard about Kari and Lila's big fight in P.E. I guess they got suspended for two days. ... Wow, I didn't know that ... a twenty-five page report? That Old Toughcracker is one strict lady.

Oh, Ashley, guess who's got a first date tonight? ... No ... no ... no ... it's Jared and Lori! ... Yes, really! She dumped Reuben because his mom made him be home by nine o'clock. ... Yeah, probably had to be home to hear his Mommy read him bedtime stories! ... Right ... with Jared she may also have a problem with bedtime stories! *(Giggles.)*

... Yes, I'm ready for tomorrow's test. ... No, I didn't pay ten bucks and buy the answers from Monte!

... Yes, I heard about Paula and Erica getting snagged in the mall for shoplifting. Can you believe it? ... Uh-huh, me, too ... I thought the mall was just for guy watchin'!

Speaking of guys ... no, I haven't actually seen him, but I heard he was a dream walking ... yes, big shoulders ... uh-huh, slim hips ... right, and biceps that make you yell out, "Oh, Mama!" ... Where did he come from? ... Omaha? Yeah, I've heard about Omaha men. Can't wait to feast these eyes on that male smorgasbord!

... You're kidding — a nose job?! And it was a graduation gift from her aunt?! Boy, that's original. ... I know, I know, Mirna's getting a Mercedes convertible — life's just not fair. ... Yes, I heard about Krista ... too bad ... uh-huh, it'll blow over in say, thirty years! Uh-oh, another call coming in ... hang on, Ashley. Hello ... oh, hi, Holly ... just a minute ... Ashley, it's Holly. Guess I'd better talk to her ... I know, I know ... it's a real drag talking to Holly ... Yes, you're right — she's such a *big gossip!*

Ten-Year Reunion

Can we talk? As I look across this sea of cap-and-gowned classmates, I wonder what will happen to us in the next ten years. Who will sink? Who will swim? Who will tread water? Who among us will achieve our goals? Who among us has goals? Who among us can *spell* goals? And we're not talking goal posts, fellas. Who will discover a much-needed cure ... Who will write novels so hot and steamy they'll set off fire alarms in bookstores across the country?

When I look at all the talent seated out there, I want to thank lots of people, starting with our teachers. First, Mrs. Gunckle, our first grade teacher, for spoon-feeding us the needed skills to read and write — true, some of you guys are stuck on the four-letter words, but that's not her fault ... and you're making some progress. Then, we must pay tribute to our eighth grade social studies teacher, Mr. Reickenborn, who taught us east from west and that a map was more than something to curl up on after eating our graham crackers! We wouldn't want to forget Mr. Small, who helped us fumigate, mutilate, and castrate 525 frogs in ninth grade science! Mr. Chilton, alias Chilto, thanks to you we learned to balance our bank accounts, add up our debts and write hot checks! And Mrs. Young, you gave us that gift which we all hold in such high esteem — a passing grade in senior English!

Now, now, don't worry ... we're not going to leave out you elective teachers — even though the rest of the staff doesn't consider you real teachers ... we do! Thanks to all the music teachers for teaching us to appreciate good music ... of course, it wasn't anything we played or sang in class! And we thank our art teachers often ... as we're tagging a wall ... or putting on body paint — artistically! And Mrs. Dominguez, thanks so much for teaching us Spanish and French ... we can now say naughty words in three languages ... and Mrs. Landry, in computer class, gave us the skills to e-mail those words across the USA! And Ms. Sanders, we'll never forget the plays you directed and wrote "just for us" ... but falling

121

off the stage and fracturing your hip carries the old saying *break a leg* too far! But thanks to all our teachers ... we are what we are because of you! Now, don't you faculty members wish you'd tried just a little harder?

But seriously, classmates, it's never too soon, you know, to start planning for the old ten-year reunion. It'll roll around before you know it. Why, it seems like only yesterday we were drooling and sucking our thumbs ... I know, I know, a couple of you guys haven't outgrown the drooling yet ... especially if a cute girl walks by, but a lot of maturing can happen in ten years ... we *hope!* Now, back to this reunion idea ... we've already buried the time capsule ... We put in Craig's old jockey shorts ... the ones he put on Clyde, the skeleton in science. We included the empty ... ah ... Kool-Aid bottle that got the golf team kicked off the greens in the state finals. We also planted our class wills and prophecies ... along with our class pictures and our *weight!* In ten years we'll see who measures up ... It'll give us all a good reason to go on crash diets a few months before the get-together! The most fun will be the Who's Who votes — Mr. Kolb, our trusty vice principal, tabulated the results and at our banquet ten years from now we'll know who we predicted to be: A. Guy most likely to be bald. B. Classmate probably living in a box. C. Best body at the age of 28. D. Best bet to be loaded ... one we'll hit up for a loan ... not one who'll have consumed too much ... Kool-Aid. E. Most likely to have his or her face on a box of Wheaties, and last F. The classmate dumped more often than the garbage by the opposite sex!

And that's all I've got to say, graduates, we did it ... They said we wouldn't, but we did it ... We got our diplomas ... Congratulations on a job well done ... Now, see ya at our ten-year reunion!

The Die's Cast

Did you ever break anything? No, I don't mean your mom's favorite vase, a nail or the football captain's heart ... I'm talking bones — did you ever break one? Well, I did — I broke my ankle ... so, you say, that's not so bad ... you should be glad it wasn't your hip ... or your neck! But the kicker is I broke it one week before Prom! Talk about timing! And miracle of miracles, I was asked by this really hot guy. I had the world's sexiest gown ... a hair appointment at La Salon ... and new Cinderella slippers (just try getting a glass slipper on a swollen tootsie encased in five pounds of plaster!) OK, I got the decorator's special — bright spurts of pinks and yellows, but it's still a cast!

It was such a stupid accident! I was climbing on a stool ... trying to get my pompoms from the top shelf in my closet ... when swish! ... the stool tipped and I fell like Humpty Dumpty ... a pompom in each hand! The doctors did put me back together again, but they added the awkward, heavy, cumbersome, colorful-though-ugly cast! And it hurt! But not nearly as much as the realization that I would be going to the prom with the coolest guy ... half barefoot, and with a cast that clashed with everything! I was sure when he found out, he'd cancel ... I waited for the call. But instead, he sent flowers and assured me I was still his date — I guess chivalry isn't dead, just fractured! But I knew we'd be sitting the whole evening ... I'd be hitting him with my crutches ... trying to fit them into his little sports car — life just isn't fair!

My friends were great ... except Kathy who said the honorable thing would be to cut Dustin loose and let him find a girl with two good feet. She was looking down at her own size sixes as she spoke — the girl has a crush on every guy I date! But she did give my conscience a little twinge, so I called Dustin and offered to let him off his disabled hook. But he played his Sir Galahad role to the end and said it would be his pleasure to escort me and my cast to the Prom.

So, the big night rolled around — Vicki and Cassie painted my toenails to match my gown; they decorated my crutches with glitter and delicate flowers; Johnny did a fabulous job with my hair; my prince was on his way ... I was all set to hobble off to the ball!

All in all, it was a fun evening. I even tried dancing ... it didn't work! So, we just talked, and I had a great time. I kept insisting that Dustin dance a little ... but he wouldn't leave my side. Kathy begged him for a dance, but he said, "When Darcy can dance again ... I'll dance!"

So, as I'm putting my scrapbook together — corsage, blank dance card, program, piece of my cast ... I'll have it to show one day to my granddaughter. I'll say, "Be careful about climbing on stools before the Prom ... otherwise you'll be limping off to the big event in a cast ... like your old granny!"

Where's My Guardian Angel When I Need Her?

My Grandma and Aunt Polly both told me from the time I was two that I had a guardian angel sitting on my shoulder taking care of me. Then, when I was six and Mama died they told me Mama was looking down, smiling over me *and* I still had that special guardian angel — two winged ones for the price of one! But now that I'm a teenager, really in need of some protection and guidance, I'm beginning to wonder if my guardian angel has gone AWOL or flown south for the winter!

There's so much going on in my life ... so many questions I need answered. Grandma does her best, but she's from another era and Aunt Polly has her hands full with her own teenagers. So, it's just you and me, Angel Mine. What should I be thinking about after I graduate? I'd like to go to college, but Gram really can't afford it. She could probably squeeze out enough to send me to cosmetology school ... I tried for a couple of scholarships, but the ones I got just don't pay enough, and Gram's social security checks and Gramps' pension can just be stretched so far. At times like this I wish for a father with a healthy bank account. Or just a father ... period! Got any answers, Guardian Angel? Can you help me pick the right numbers in the lottery? What good's a guardian angel if she can't help me out from time to time?

And, now that I have your attention, what am I going to do about Brett? I can't keep saying no forever. He's really putting the pressure on me ... can you help me out with that situation? I'm sure an angel wouldn't want me to give in ... I don't want to end up like my mom raising a child alone. Sure, I like Brett, but I don't hear bells ring; my heart doesn't do flip-flops when he enters the room. I may be old-fashioned, but I want bells, stars, music — the whole enchilada! So, you agree with that, huh? Somehow I knew you would. I get the feeling that you think I should cut the cord ... set Brett free. I'll miss him, but I can do that.

What's this? *(Picks up letter.)* ... It's a letter from K-State. You know

I really wanted to be a Wildcat ... probably just another reject. Hummm, what? Listen to this ... I can't believe it! I qualified for a *full* scholarship ... everything paid! And they'll help me find a part-time job! I don't know what to say. Wait till I tell Gram! And, Guardian Angel, thanks ... and keep sitting on my shoulder, will ya?

Girls or Guys

Body Parts

I know it's a strange thing to wonder about ... but I'm a teenager and I'm supposed to have out-of-this-world thoughts! But did you ever notice how some people have such stupefying body parts? OK, OK ... I'm a kook! But it's true. Take, for example, that honker on Mr. Classen, our science teacher. I mean ... I've seen big noses, but this guy's schnoz looks like the tip of the iceberg that took down the Titanic! And Mrs. Snipple, the librarian. She has four chins! When they were passing them out, I guess she just kept going ... and going ... and going.

I know you've all noticed these little imperfections ... OK, so some of you are just too shy or too nice to speak up. But sometimes ... things just need to be brought to the surface ... spelled out! Take, for example, those people who are *all* eyebrows — one long, worm-like strip across their forehead! And I don't even want to talk about zits, birthmarks or crow's feet! I do want to discuss lips, though. Old Lady Murphy has *none* — I mean, *none* ... just a line below her nose ... if there ever were lips, they're all sucked in ... not exactly chicken lips, but close ... dried up ... like her personality!

Hair is always good for a laugh ... and ranges anywhere from blue-haired curly tops to chrome domes! Ever notice to what lengths old guys will go to try to cover a bald spot? And old gals! They spend millions to be permed, frosted, toned, braided, clipped ... and still many look like hurricane leftovers.

The body itself is good material for a stand-up comedian. I know we like to pick on chubby people ... and it's *not* fair ... but somehow poking fun at anorexic, skeletal bodies doesn't get many laughs. But you must admit there are lots of strange-shaped bodies running around out there ... shapes that make a living for cartoonists! Just looking at legs can give a person the chuckles. And it's not just the short sausage-link thighs, but also the hairy legs, the toothpick legs, and legs so bowed Amtrac could go between them! Then, the feet — you just don't see too many good-lookin' tootsies. It's the toes that make the foot. Those short, curled little piggies going to market are good for a belly laugh. But it's the long, finger-like toesies that I think are weird! They can pick up underwear thrown on the floor, grasp a brush to paint the walls or even flip a burger!

I don't even want to talk about the lumps, bumps and knobs found on the average human body, but I'm very interested in the specks and spots! No, I'm not going to make a big deal about those rust spots on old ladies' hands and (probably) other places — but I am fascinated by freckles! Where do those spots before your eyes come from? You don't see too many babies in hospital nurseries with those dot-to-dot marks! Why do some people have none ... others (often redheads) have light sprinkles across the nose ... and others inherit a freckle factory?

See, there's just so much to observe and question about human frailties. So, now maybe you can begin to understand my fascination with ... my quandary over ... *body parts!*

Caught in the Middle

I think it would be great to be the oldest child. My older sister Kisa gets all the perks — because she's more mature ... has a good head on her shoulders ... has more baby pictures! Then, it would also be nice to be the baby. Mom's so worn out, busy and old from raising Kisa and myself, she lets Jenny run free! And, of course, both my sisters can wrap Dad around their first- and last-born fingers!

So you see where that leaves me   smack in the middle of Miss Maturity and Baby Face! I'm a nobody — caught in the middle. I know in some things middle is better — the good stuff's in the center of the Oreo ... the filling of a sandwich is what it's all about ... we all dive for the middle of a Twinkie ... but this doesn't hold true with kids. It's kind of like middle school — a wasteland!

I don't know why my folks didn't stop having kids after I was born ... then I could have been the youngest ... had a real place in the family tree. Then I wouldn't have cared so much when Kisa gets a bigger allowance ... when she gets a car ... when she gets to stay out later and has fewer household chores. I wouldn't mind then because nobody would expect so much from me, because I'd be the Baby. Or, better yet, if Mom'd given Kisa up for adoption, I'd have been the number one kid ... the one with three baby books, millions of videos, and enough pictures to fill the Grand Canyon! If I were the older child, I'd be more tolerant of Jenny ... I wouldn't mind that everyone hugs her more and gives her more gifts at Christmas.

Now Grandma Beard could have lightened my middle load if she'd spoiled me a little. I do, after all, carry a family middle name in her honor. A good payback for this burden would have been a little extra attention — to make up for Mom's worshipful allegiance to Kisa and Dad's ga-ga devotion to Goo-Goo Baby! But Gram's too busy with her bridge clubs, community meetings, and charity work to give a helping hand to the middle kid — doesn't she know charity begins at home?

131

So, since Grandma's no help ... since Mom didn't quit birthin' babies after I was born ... and since she didn't put Kisa in an orphanage ... I'm still stuck in the middle. Is it any wonder I had an imaginary friend that always paid attention to me ... told me how smart and special I was! I'm only having two children! There'll be an older child (that special-place-in-a-mother's-heart-first-child) and (the light of Daddy's-life) Baby! I won't be bringing another fellow sufferer into this world ... absolutely ... positively ... *No middle child!*

Computers Byte

My biggest enemy in this crazy mixed-up school system is a computer. It tells how many times I've been tardy or skipped class; when my next shots are due; how many books I've got overdue at the library and what classes I'm flunking. I think the whole computer concept was designed to snoop and snitch on kids' lives! I saw a teacher pull my biographical information once — (to see if I was for real, or just a visiting alien) and I swear that machine had my family history traced back to the pilgrims! Talk about invasion of privacy! Why do they have to know my blood type? Are they expecting trouble, or is Count Dracula lurking somewhere behind the stacks of computer paper? And the files in the office — they read like a prison printout — who fought whom, who got detentions and why, who threw grapes in the lunchroom (purple or green)! And these files follow you for life ... someone said they're used to write your obituary! My dad says school was better in the "good old days." When a kid did something wrong, he got his butt whipped and it was forgotten ... did away with all the paperwork and record keeping!

But we've all been trained and retrained to use these computers since kindergarten; it really cut down on the nap and cracker break! The bad thing is, we learn on one machine and then the next year they've changed equipment, and we only recognize the start-up button!

It's true we love the computer games — they help us with eye-to-hand coordination, make us think faster ... and let's face it, we like the challenge, especially in the blood-and-guts games! And we like to scope the net and find out tidbits about topics of interest: cars, celebrities, wrestling. We appreciate how much easier it is to find information for a report or speech. So, I guess it's not *all* bad!

But for the most part, I'd like school better without them ... I don't like one teacher e-mailing another that "Tommy's in a bad mood today ... watch out!" Maybe Tommy just hates that one teacher and respects the others ... but they'll all crack down on Tommy ... teachers always stick together, even when one's wrong! I also don't like that they've taken the old shop and home ec. classes and now have computer modules. I think a guy or girl would learn more making a lamp or baking a cherry pie or sewing up a pair of PJs than watching another computer screen for an hour!

I know we're living in a world of technology now ... and a person has to either join in or get left behind. But I still say — just because it's new, just because every other school has it, just because it costs ten zillion taxpayers' dollars — doesn't mean it's good. Well, I'm winding down, running out of facts ... should have gone to the computer! See? It's inescapable ... and that's why I say computers byte!

Don't Be Pet-ty

I really think the good people — the soft-hearted humans can be identified because they're pet owners. Have you ever noticed that sour, down-on-lifers never buy Cat Chow, Alpo or birdseed? I really think you can tell more about a person's inner self by the paw prints on her carpet than by using those fancy ink blot tests!

Now I know some people go overboard — twenty-seven cats in a one-room apartment can make a lot of litter! And, too, herds of Dalmatians will spoil the flower garden, the rug, not to mention the neighbors' sleep. But taken in small doses the canine and feline are faithful friends — ones who will still lick your feet when the rest of the world thinks you're scum!

But simple pets are not for everyone ... some people go for the exotic. My friend down the block got a parrot — J.R. chewed up the pillows, curtains, the *cat* ... and learned only four-letter cuss words! He became such an embarrassment when the PTA ladies and minister visited ... they had to give the bird to an ex-sailor! My old friend Chris begged and begged for a pet ... his mom was allergic (or said she was) to anything that purred, jumped on your leg, swam in bowls, sat on a perch, or had purses made from its skin! She finally gave in and let Chris have a turtle ... because it didn't bark or have to be taken monthly to the groomers or produce hairballs. Well, Chris and Toodles became close friends ... Chris learned all about turtles ... and talked to him in sign language. But, alas, one day Toodles disappeared ... they searched high and low ... put up posters ... offered rewards ... but no Toodles! Six months later, Chris was doing his yearly room-clean (He was not a Mr. Tidybowl!) and under the bed he found a turtle shell — it was stuck to the floor with a big wad of bubble gum!

Rabbits and white mice make interesting companions ... and goldfish are so relaxing to watch ... if you're not prone to seasickness ... and they'll never bring any complaints from the neighbors! Another kid I

135

know has a pet skunk — Pepy's been de-odorized ... but he still has a certain stigma ... and he's never invited to any pet parties! Greg's popular with the girls because he owns Iggie, a box-trained iguana. Other people have great luck with parakeets or canaries — their soothing chirping could quiet your nerves after listening to teachers yak all day! Then, of course, if you're really adventuresome ... I suggest a snake! This one really depends on how fearless your mom is — faint-hearted moms usually veto this interesting pet!

Now I, myself, love them all — that's why my dream is to one day own a pet store! Then, I can play with the furry, slimy, creepy, cuddly creatures all I want and still make a few bucks! I seriously encourage all of you good people out there to invest in a pet ... you'll never be sorry! In fact, you owe it to yourself ... 'cause no matter how many legs they have, you can never have too many friends!

Down with School Uniforms

You're never going to believe this — starting next year our high school has to wear uniforms! We'll look like inmates ... inmates in khaki instead of black and white stripes! It's all the teachers' fault; they say we're out of control — too much gang insignia and graffiti on our T-shirts. Do they really think dressing us like little clones will help our behavior? *I don't think so!* In fact, it's going to make us all so mad we'll act worse.

I know, I know, I've heard the Board of Education president spout all the statistics from other schools — school violence decreased, referrals cut in half, no class distinction because cliques, gangs, and preps all dress alike. It'll be hard to tell the rich kids from the poor ones (unless you observe the student parking lot and see who loads into the expensive wheels). I'll give the PTA ladies some credit; they fought against the Mighty Uniform sentence, arguing that kids need to express their creativity and identity through their wardrobe. They accused the school officials of trying to rip off the students' freedom of expression. I'm sure it will add to the drop-out rate — guys look better in coveralls and chef's aprons ... and girls will head for short waitress skirts and Candy Stripers' outfits! I think the founding fathers would have added it to the Bill of Rights if they'd realized that some out-of-control administrators were going to force feed school uniforms down the throats of every teenager in our city! I know Moses was a sport and his eleventh commandment would be: "Thou shalt not force teens to wear dorky, look-alike school clothes!"

And what about the teachers and principals? Are they going to have to wear this fashion-reject uniform gear? It's mostly their fault, so I think these instructors of higher learning should spend their small clothing allowance on prison garb also.

Well, as Mom always says, "You can't fight City Hall," ... but you don't have to like their laws. As creative as kids are, we'll think of something — the girls will jazz their outfits with outlandish jewelry ... garage sales will be hard hit! We'll all wear weird, wild socks and shoes, and nothing's been said about neckties — the more grotesque the better! Then, too, there's hair style ... and color ... and wild makeup! So, we may be wearing their low-class, loose-fitting, stupid army surplus uniforms, but we're *never, never* going to like it!

Drop-in or Dropout?

Drop-in or drop out of school, that is the question. Whether 'tis nobler to hang in there when everything's so screwed up, or just hang it up!

It's just getting too hard ... Mom bailed out two years ago; she got tired of my little brother Sean and me fighting ... and, of course, there was Dad's drinking. I'll never forgive her for leaving me behind. She swore she'd send for us when she found a good job and got settled. Well, she not only found a job, she found Ken ... who, it seems, wants no part of Sean or me. So, we're stuck here. Keeping Sean in lunch money, clean clothes and making sure he does his homework is a full-time job — Mom's job, not *mine!* Sometimes I don't blame her for bailing out and other times I'm bitter ... it was her duty to stick it out till she got us both through school. We didn't ask for any of this; it's not our fault she married a loser. But it's always the kids who pay for adult errors — it's just not fair!

I do have an out ... I don't *have* to stay. Mom showed me how easy it is to ignore responsibility and think only of myself. I could get a job in an office; I've taken hours of computer classes and I do look older — being on my own at seventeen has made me grow up fast ... too fast. I don't really have any friends at school; I didn't have time to try out for sports ... had to get home to Sean. And I could never invite a friend to my house, because who knew when Dad would appear and if he'd be drunk or sober. So, I became a loner. I had chances to date — I do have Mom's curly, dark hair and great skin, but who'd watch Sean, and what kind of scene could I expect if Dad was here when my date picked me up? So, it's just been easier to go solo. I do try to see that Sean has some buddies; I take them out for pizza and bowling. I see that he makes it to Little League and Scouts. I don't want him to be a social misfit like me.

So, some days I just think I'll forget school ... too much of a struggle. Then again, the counselor says she can get me a scholarship right here

139

in the city if I stick it out. I've made it this far, my grades are good, and I've always wanted to be a nurse. It's only a few more months ... maybe a miracle will happen. Dad's in rehab again, maybe this time it'll take. Maybe Mom will dump Ken and send for us. I don't know ... maybe I'll keep at it; I know a diploma will make a lot of difference ... but why does it all have to be so hard?

Family Eat-Outs

I suppose some of you really like to eat out with your relatives. I see Ward and June Cleaver families in restaurants — they are dressed up, using Emily Post manners, and yet having fun! I watch these families not having food fights! It almost makes me want to join them — adopt a new close-knit eating group.

'Cause, ... well ... my family can't go out in public with forks in their hands! Now, they can make it through a church service, manage parent-teacher conferences, take in a movie (if popcorn and Milk Duds are forgotten), attend a funeral, or fly in an airplane (if only finger foods are served), but they can't go *out* to eat together! It's not just my immediate family we're talking about either — this eating disorder stretches throughout *every* branch of my family tree.

Uncle Pete is banned from *every* restaurant in our city ... they finally caught on to his smuggling — worms, wads of hair, old teeth, rocks, etc., into places and after he'd almost finished his meal he'd make a big scene. He'd call for the manager ... show him the unmentionable intruder ... it worked for years. Uncle Pete ate lots of free meals.

Aunt Lucy isn't one of my favorite dining partners, either. She skips around the room asking to taste other people's entrées ... she takes her own fork and can stab a shrimp before any plate owner has a chance to say no! On a good night, Lucy won't actually have to order ... her little snitching tummy will be full of pilfered plunder! Are you beginning to get the picture?

We can't feed my twin brothers in public — they're too jealous of the other's food if they don't order identical meals, and if they *do,* they'll fight over who got the bigger bun, riper tomato, most mustard!

I'll never step foot inside another eating establishment with my father, either. He always thinks he's being cheated ... goes over the bill like he was an IRS spy — gets his calculator out and re-adds everything ... and then consistently scrimps on the tip! Mom's not too bad unless there's a baby ... in a highchair ... anywhere in the eatery. She can radar in on baby powder, and she coochy-coos the kid throughout the meal. (We've all agreed *not* to give her grandchildren!)

And the list goes on — Grandpa pinches the waitresses, Cousin Tammy steals the tips, Great Aunt Flossie sends everything back, and my sister combs her hair and files her nails at the table while flirting with everyone over seventeen. So now you see why I have food phobias ... why I think handicapped parking in front of cafes should be saved for my family! It's obvious now why we do cover-dish and carry-out for all reunions. 'Cause without a doubt, my family is definitely dining dysfunctional!

Fast Food Junkie

I want to eat right ... food from the basic food groups, but all the good gooey stuff keeps getting in my stomach first! I'll admit it — I'm hooked on junk food. I love anything that comes shootin' out the window of a fast food place. I want to "drive in for a change" and feed my face. I want "hot eats, cool treats" and I want them quick! Whatever that little Taco Tico dog's sellin' — I'm eatin'! If it's under the arches, it's first rate to me, and I do "deserve a break today!" My digestive system's very much in sync with burgers, fries, pizza, chili dogs and milkshakes in all flavors — I really flip over the new coconut cream pie and banana meringue!

My mom's really on my case all the time about nutritious foods — I ask you, what's so great about veggies? I know all about vitamins and fiber. My mom tried all these creative recipes to trick me into eating my greens. There isn't enough cheese or dip in the universe to disguise the disgusting taste of broccoli! Occasionally, I'll munch a carrot just to make Mom happy and to do my Bugs Bunny routine — "Eh, what's up, Doc?" Now, Popeye can keep his vile old spinach — I don't care how strong it makes him. I'll eat a little salad at Grandma's — she's loaded and I don't want to be expelled from the will for refusing to chew a little roughage!

I don't care what the authorities say, school lunch falls under the category of Junk Food — more junk than food! Even the plastic turkey they serve for Thanksgiving and Christmas dinners is guaranteed to gag a giraffe ... and that's a whole lot of gaggin'! But my folks think the cafeteria slop is really healthy and won't hear of me taking my lunch. (I would much prefer to pack my Mighty Mouse lunch box with gut-fillers like Twinkies, chips and Snickers.) But instead, I swallow all those foul-tasting carbos the lunch ladies dish out — starch plopped so high on our plates it's a wonder we can bend our knees to scrape out our scraps ... and say a little prayer that we won't die of food poisoning!

It's after school that I get to the good stuff — it's a parade of teenage food junkies heading for the drive-ins, the pizza places, and the take-out joints. We all need a fast food fix to erase the vile taste of school lunch. A few bites of real food turns the tide — our stomachs are coated with enough grease to get through our moms' wholesome dinners.

When I grow up ... become mature ... can vote and support myself (With a little help from Grandma's will ... remember, I swallow salad at her place), I'll eat whatever I want. If I want a Big Mac for breakfast — so be it! If a banana split hits the hunger spot in my tummy — I'm splittin' a banana! My fridge will runneth over with fatty, sugary, unhealthy foodstuffs! I can't wait till I'm in charge of my own life ... my own soul ... my own stomach!

My mother got me a book called *Eating Healthy* — all about colon cancer, clogged arteries, heart attack, high blood pressure — sometimes I read a little of it as I munch my chips. I guess it is food for thought!

If Wishes
Could Come True

If I could find a lamp with a wish-granting genie, if my Fairy Godmother would suddenly appear with her magic wand, if I saw a hundred falling stars and could make a wish on every star, I would have a loooong wish list!

I'd forget about wanting mountains of money. (Though what kid couldn't use a few bucks in the old bank account?) I'd never ask for fabulous vacations or fancy cars. (But I wouldn't mind a new set of tires for my old Toyota.) I wouldn't want to waste one precious wish on selfish, materialistic possessions. No, the world is in dire need of important, life-saving wishes. First, I'd wish for cures for all dreaded diseases that are wiping out family members, friends and teens around the world. I've watched people I love suffer from cancer, diabetes, hepatitis, AIDS, and many other ailments that keep them from enjoying life to the fullest. Next, I'd stamp out greed — some people just can't get enough money, fast enough cars, big enough houses, good-looking enough women or men. Then I'd cancel all prejudice — stamping out hatred. I'm talking *all* prejudice — racial, sexual, political ... you name it, I want it stopped. Too many kids are suffering from it right in this school. Who hasn't snickered when a heavy student walks by, or poked a little fun at a nerd minding his own business, or pulled a demeaning prank on a self-conscious guy who might be gay? Who hasn't cracked a few jokes at the expense of somebody in Special Education or a social misfit? If you can answer these questions truthfully and say, "Not me!" then you are truly a rare person and we need more of your type to change the status quo — making nobody an outcast ... getting rid of the hate that builds up within these outsiders until something like Columbine happens. I know a lot of this prejudice comes from right at home. Well, it's too late to reshape our folks' thinking, but it's not too late for us to change our own attitudes. So, with or without the wand ... even if Jeannie doesn't come out of her bottle to help us ... let's help ourselves ... let's reach down inside our souls and throw out all the hate, all the prejudice, all the I'm-better-than-you-attitudes and just make this school, this country, a better place ... for *all* people.

‑o Be a
‑hool Teacher

Call me crazy, call me strange, call me lobotomized, but I want to be a teacher — and I'm not through yet — I want to teach at a middle school! I know, I know, I've seen the look of disbelief, of sympathy, of terror on people's faces when I 'fess up to this deep-seated desire of mine. My friends wonder if they should be running around with such a moron, my folks think it's just a phase and I'll outgrow it, my teachers say I'm shell-shocked from too much homework and school lunches! But I know I'm not insane, I know I won't outgrow it, I know I want to teach in-between-agers — the age at which most adults agree these almost-adolescents should be locked in cages and fed raw meat!

What can I say? My years at middle school were the best in my life. In grade school we were too busy learning to write and made the highest reading group. In high school we're all stressed out on how many extra-curricular activities we could rack up and our GPA. But in middle school everything was more relaxed ... the emphasis was on teamwork, no competition, no tryouts — everybody played in sports, everybody had a chance to succeed. And the teachers were tops — oddballs, yes, but normal teachers couldn't survive very long in that habitat. We had teachers who sang our spelling words to us ... teachers who dressed up like characters from history to teach the lesson. (You'd never see a stuffed-shirt high school pro teach history that way — they only know "read and outline the next chapter.") These middle school teachers were not hesitant to load our whole team into buses and take us on all-day field trips ... you see, they're fearless — Rambos with chalkdust on their butts! They gave us every opportunity to discover our talents. Besides the required core courses, we took exploratory wheel classes — art, foreign language, technology/shop, computer, family living/home ec, vocal/instrumental music, and my favorite, expressive arts. (We got to act up in this drama class and really express ourselves in strange hats, wigs and costumes.) So we came out well-rounded kids; kids who knew how to sew a pair of boxer shorts, make a wooden candleholder, create artistic art projects. We became kids who knew computers and other languages, and kids who weren't afraid to show off on stage. Talk about an education!

I mentioned the outgoing, martyr-like faculty ... well, the administration did its part, too. Yes, these principals kept us in line by being firm, yet also leaving us with a little dignity. They, too, like the faculty, had a sense of humor ... the number one requirement for anyone dealing with these early teens. And I really think God's created a special place in heaven for middle school teachers. What a wild place it must be, 'cause nobody has as much fun or is more caring than this crazy bunch of educators. So, do you still think I'm insane for wanting to be one?

Just Desserts

I'm sitting here in detention ... society's outcast. Oh sure, the bars are missing, but my body knows it's in solitary confinement ... no contact with the outside world, no friendly smile from the opposite sex to lighten my sentence, no word of encouragement from the bailiff, no bribing the jury.

How did I get here, you want to know? What road did I choose that led to this after-school detention room? Well, it's a long story. You see, I have taken on the quest of exploring all forms of teacher punishment ... and I've made it a personal involvement! Yes, I've experienced all forms of the educational system's disciplinary action ... and though it's true I have no physical scars on my backside, who knows the trauma my psyche has suffered.

It's no secret that all teachers and administrators take college classes in gettin' even. Oh sure, they doctor up the course title calling it something fancy like Behavioral Tactics ... but a little detective work would, I'm sure, uncover the author of the required text as A. Hitler. And a little more research would prove that most educators made A-plusses in this required course!

I know, I know, you all have memories of that soft-spoken, white-haired instructor who "made a difference" in your life! But under hypnosis I'd bet my next ten detention slips you'd remember that same "angel of adjectives" carried a ruler in her hip pocket and knew how to use it! It's the secondary teachers who have perfected the fine art of student torture. They're bitter ... and because their systems are filled with academic acid, they take their disappointments out on poor, innocent students ... like myself. OK, to be fair, sometimes I deserve some sort of reprimand ... but a gentle reminder might jar me back into being the ideally behaved student ... at least it's worth a shot before literally throwing the book at me! Now, the really lucky felons get out-of-school suspension ... but I've only been dealt that hand once ... and must confess it wasn't the picnic I supposed it to be. You see, my folks are of the old school … which translated means they gave me lowly tasks to do, a grounding that out-lasted puberty … so I never want to taste that kind of freedom again!

Our school has a "no weapon" policy, and yet they turn Ms. Crankyface loose in the classroom with a dozen rulers … she breaks two or three a week … and an equal number of student's spirits! And that you'll-never-amount-to-anything stare the coach casts on all the benchwarmers falls in the lethal category! And anybody who knows Old Lady Sharptalk knows what a dangerous weapon lies behind her cutting remarks hurled at us with her razor-sharp tongue! And these are the same instructors who put on their false happy faces at parent-teacher conferences and PTA meetings! It's a mixed-up world, isn't it?

So, as I continue my study of the punishment policy in our fair school system … I will dedicate my masterpiece to all unfortunate students who suffer unfairly at the hands of ruthless, power-hungry educators! Catch ya later, the warden's back! And I've still got thirty minutes to serve. Since I did the crime, I guess I'll just shut up and serve my time!

Lucky Charms

Do you go around ladders instead of under them? Do you run a mile so a black cat won't walk in front of your path? If you spill salt, do you quickly throw a handful over your shoulder? If you can say no to these questions, you're one lucky kid! If, on the other hand, you must truthfully nod to any of these inquiries, you've been raised by someone with some quirky beliefs — and you, my friend, are superstitious!

It's hard to get through life without some superstitions. Maybe you have a few and don't realize it. For instance, most people have lucky numbers — and use them weekly in the lottery. I loved six till I found out it was a "devil number!" Are you one of the guilty parties who tromped a clover patch to pieces looking for that four-leafer? Do you make a wish on every falling star? Do you jump cracks in the sidewalk to save your mother's backbone? Do you skip school on Friday the thirteenth (and any other day you feel lucky)? And how many bunnies bit the dust to provide all those lucky rabbits' feet? And speaking of feet, how many horses lost their shoes so they could be nailed above the door — ends up ... so the luck doesn't run out!

See, this thing is bigger than you thought. Our football coach has a lucky ten dollar bill he found when his team made it to state playoffs ... he makes the whole team kiss it before each game. (We keep losing anyway, maybe he needs to up it to a twenty!) Kevin has a cross that never leaves his scrawny neck ... brides hobble down the aisle with a penny in their shoes and something old, new, borrowed, and blue hung someplace on their veiled bodies! And I'll just bet somebody you know wears an angel pin — they're all the rage ... a guardian angel to watch over you. My mom put one on my bulletin board, and Grandma never leaves home without one ... on her bra! But then you must realize my family has a history of insanity. Superstition runs rampant in our genes! Great Grandma Parker will get up out of her wheelchair to stop an empty rocking chair from rocking — sure sign that somebody in the family will

151

die! Aunt Flo will throw another potato in the pot if she drops her dishrag — a proven fact that company's on the way! Auntie Esther keeps her eye peeled for a lady's hem turned up — upon finding one, she gives it a hearty smackeroo for luck ... and the bewildered owner is left with slobber skirt! If you see a hearse and don't hold a button — you can kiss someone you love good-bye ... buy funeral clothes! And nobody ... I mean, nobody tells ... before breakfast ... if they dreamed of somebody's death ... 'cause if they do, the star of that dream becomes a member of the dearly departed! Also, if it rains when the sun's shining, our whole family wears rain hats the next day at the exact time of yesterday's downpour! If you dream of the dead — you'll hear from the living. And the roof of our family car is covered with grubby handprints ... evidence of hopeful hands pressing the ceiling ... while making a wish ... when going through a tunnel! It's hard to get through a day without being affected by these folklorish beliefs. And Granny says if you want to see superstition in full bloom, go to Las Vegas where everyone has a technique ... a style ... a lucky charm — all based on superstition. I'm headin' there when I'm old enough to throw a few coins in the video poker machines. Of course, I'll have my lucky frog foot in my pocket!

Preps Get All the Breaks

Life's just not fair, but I guess nobody said it was gonna be. But I just wish it would even out a little. Take, for instance, the way the Preps, the in-crowd, the Jocks are treated. It's not just in this school — it's a universal expectation ... these special people get the royal treatment and the rest of us get the shaft!

Oh sure, there's not a teacher worth his chalkdust who'd admit it, but deep in their little addled minds, they know it's true — the popular kids get by with murder and the rest of us lowlives get punished for every little infringement ... to the full extent of the law! All a Jock has to do is smile at a female teacher, or laugh at a coach's stupid jokes and all is forgiven. The popular girls, cheerleaders leading the pack, wiggle their cutsie behinds and have a license to take over any class. These chosen ones know they'll be class officers, yearbook editors, Prom Queens, Who's Who nominees, Honor Society winners, float riders, debaters, and have, of course, leads in all the school plays. Remaining school achievement crumbs are scattered sparingly among the common masses.

Don't get me wrong, this class system is nothing new. I'm sure Moses wouldn't have been alone on that mountain reading tablets if he'd been one of the preppie people! Abe wouldn't have been studying law by candlelight if he'd been a super Jock! Hitler might not have caused all that havoc if he'd felt like he belonged to the in-crowd!

I'm not saying these teenage idols have a perfect life; I know they have their problems the same as we commoners do — material things don't make people happy. You have to be happy within yourself. But, it'd sure make our day if these bigger-than-life winners would just take the time to nod or say hi to the little people. After all, we're all in this together — everyone deserves a chance regardless of his income, wardrobe or clique!

About the Author

Shirley Ullom is a speech/drama teacher in the Dodge City, Kansas school system. Writing is her hobby — she writes the plays her students perform. (Many of them are in the Contemporary Drama Service catalog, as is her first book, *Get in the Act!* — a popular teenage publication containing monologs, dialogs and skits.) She is a member of the Kansas Authors Club, where she has won many writing awards and presented writing seminars. She has created writing clubs for students, helping many teenagers get published. She has also written articles for various magazines and humorous lines for stand-up comics ... including Joan Rivers.

Order Form

Meriwether Publishing Ltd.
P.O. Box 7710
Colorado Springs, CO 80933
Telephone: (719) 594-4422
Website: www.meriwetherpublishing.com

Please send me the following books:

_____	**Tough Acts to Follow #BK-B237**	**$14.95**
	by Shirley Ullom	
	75 monologs for teens	
_____	**Get in the Act! #BK-B104**	**$14.95**
	by Shirley Ullom	
	Monologs, dialogs, and skits for teens	
_____	**Tight Spots #BK-B233**	**$14.95**
	by Diana Howie	
	True-to-life monolog characterizations for student actors	
_____	**Winning Monologs for Young Actors #BK-B127**	**$14.95**
	by Peg Kehret	
	Honest-to-life monologs for young actors	
_____	**Encore! More Winning Monologs for Young Actors #BK-B144**	**$14.95**
	by Peg Kehret	
	More honest-to-life monologs for young actors	
_____	**The Flip Side #BK-B221**	**$14.95**
	by Heather H. Henderson	
	64 point-of-view monologs for teens	
_____	**Acting Natural #BK-B133**	**$14.95**
	by Peg Kehret	
	Honest-to-life monologs, dialogs, and playlets for teens	

These and other fine Meriwether Publishing books are available at your local bookstore or direct from the publisher. Use the handy order form on this page.

Name: _____

Organization name: _____

Address: _____

City: _____ State: _____

Zip: _____ Phone: _____

❑ **Check Enclosed**

❑ **Visa or MasterCard #** _____

Signature: _____   *Expiration date:* _____

(*required for Visa/MasterCard orders*)

Colorado residents: Please add 3% sales tax.
Shipping: Include $2.75 for the first book and 50¢ for each additional book ordered.

❑ *Please send me a copy of your complete catalog of books and plays.*

Order Form

Meriwether Publishing Ltd.
P.O. Box 7710
Colorado Springs, CO 80933
Telephone: (719) 594-4422
Website: www.meriwetherpublishing.com

Please send me the following books:

_____ **Tough Acts to Follow #BK-B237** $14.95
by Shirley Ullom
75 monologs for teens

_____ **Get in the Act! #BK-B104** $14.95
by Shirley Ullom
Monologs, dialogs, and skits for teens

_____ **Tight Spots #BK-B233** $14.95
by Diana Howie
True-to-life monolog characterizations for student actors

_____ **Winning Monologs for Young Actors** $14.95
#BK-B127
by Peg Kehret
Honest-to-life monologs for young actors

_____ **Encore! More Winning Monologs for** $14.95
Young Actors #BK-B144
by Peg Kehret
More honest-to-life monologs for young actors

_____ **The Flip Side #BK-B221** $14.95
by Heather H. Henderson
64 point-of-view monologs for teens

_____ **Acting Natural #BK-B133** $14.95
by Pcg Kehret
Honest-to-life monologs, dialogs, and playlets for teens

These and other fine Meriwether Publishing books are available at
your local bookstore or direct from the publisher. Use the handy
order form on this page.

Name: _____

Organization name: _____

Address: _____

City: _____ State: _____

Zip: _____ Phone: _____

❑ **Check Enclosed**

❑ **Visa or MasterCard #** _____

Signature: _____   Expiration date: _____

           (required for Visa/MasterCard orders)

Colorado residents: Please add 3% sales tax.
Shipping: Include $2.75 for the first book and 50¢ for each additional book ordered.

❑ *Please send me a copy of your complete catalog of books and plays.*